MW00910519

MOTORBOOKS
INTERNATIONAL

This edition published in 2003 by Motorbooks International, an imprint of
MBI Publishing Company, Galtier Plaza, Suite 200, 380 Jackson Street,
St. Paul, MN 55101-3885 USA

© 2002-2003, Octagon Motorsport for SEP Editrice

Motorbooks International titles are also available at discounts in bulk quantity
for industrial or sales-promotional use. For details write to Special Sales
Manager at Motorbooks International Wholesalers & Distributors, Galtier
Plaza, Suite 200, 380 Jackson Street, St. Paul, MN 55101-3885 USA.

Library of Congress Cataloging-in-Publication Data Available

ISBN 0-7603-1558-2
Printed in Italy

superbike
2002-2003

SUMMARY

4

Texts and design
CLAUDIO PORROZZI

Photographs
FABRIZIO PORROZZI
STEFANO GADDA
TINO MARTINO
ALESSANDRO PIREDDA

Graphic design and layout
DARIO IACOPONI

Printed in November 2002

WELCOME

I still have Imola in my mind, my heart and my eyes.

I will never easily be able to forget the final round of the 2002 World Superbike Championship, either as a fan of motorcycle racing or as the President of the FIM. At Imola sport triumphed over everything and everyone, and that day everyone forgot everything in order to give themselves body and soul to this sport through its magnificent heroes.

The Motorcycling Federation, Superbike International, the constructors, the sponsors, the riders have all worked hard together, year after year, and will continue to do so to reach one main aim: to witness the triumph of the sport where winners and losers, modern-day cavaliers, shake each other's hand and embrace each other at the end of breath-taking duels.

The World Superbike Championship is all this and more; technology, research, commercial interests, human and sporting values all merge together to form a single unity and this unity once again is the body, the soul and the life of the World Superbike Championship.
We will work our hardest to make sure that spectacles like the one at Imola offered by the World Superbike Championship will be repeated over and over again and continue to excite us like they have so far.

Ad majora and here's to the road!

Francesco Zerbi, FIM President

SPEECHLESS!

There is no longer any need for adjectives or definitions to describe Superbike: all you have to do is experience it, especially in a season like 2002, when the excitement only died down at the end of the final race.

Superbike is alive and kicking however also off the track both for the fans, who have the opportunity to meet their idols and the bikes of their dreams, and for those involved in the championship.

The climate within Superbike is so congenial that no one flees from contact and everyone is happy to take part in a large community festival. Not to mention the technical contents of a category that sees production-based bikes involved at the highest competitive level possible, where they succeed in expressing interesting results (just look at the lap times and top speeds!). And the supporting categories for Superbike are just as valid both from a technical and sporting point of view, starting with the surprising Supersport, in addition to Superside and the competitive Superstock training formula. To sum up, in this book we would like to present the wonderful world of the WSBK Championship: welcome to four-stroke heaven!

PERSISTENCE OF VISION

It's almost fitting that the finish to the 2002 World Superbike year was one of the best ever in the 15 season history of Superbike racing on a global scale. There have been last minute dramas in yesteryear (witness 1998, for example, with three riders capable of winning it outright before the last race of the year), but in terms of a championship result being turned around from the mid-season expected outcome, few campaigns can rival the end of 2002 SBK duel.

In the first 70% of the season it was Troy Bayliss who felt affinity for the top step of the podium like it was his third child, with the reigning champ monopolizing the top step on 14 occasions in 17 attempts. By race one at Laguna Seca he was a monumental 58 points ahead of the second place man Colin Edwards, despite a couple of small mishaps.

Nine races later, and nine more wins for Edwards, the world title had been awarded to the American and not the Australian, to the man who never gave up, from the team that never gave up, even when they felt that they had no chance of winning by their own efforts alone and may just have been going through the motions.

Persistence of vision takes on a whole new meaning after this SBK year.

It was also the most tyre-influenced season imaginable, with the other manufacturers gasping in the wake of the big money, big technology effort from Michelin.

Hence the huge points gap between the two top men, Edwards and Bayliss, and most of the rest.

Semi-privateer Neil Hodgson was easily the next best man, Aprilia's Noriyuki Haga deserves mention for some strong rides, Ducati L's Ben Bostrom was a fleeting shadow of his occasionally brilliant self in 2001, and Michelin runner Ruben Xaus resident on either podium or gravel trap, depending on the day.

The four-cylinder machines? Will return to fight the next world war with bigger caliber ammunition.

The story of the year may have ended up being about two men, one tyre choice and one engine design philosophy but Edwards and Bayliss‚Äô private battle was every bit as competitive and compelling at the end as a six rider fight would have been mid-season.

Not the best year of racing, but arguably the best end of year.

Gordon Ritchie

This has been a unique, extraordinary season. In the history of motorcycle racing, it often happens that one rider or one motorbike dominates to such a point that the championship itself loses all of its interest. In 2002 we were privileged to have two great champions, each of whom was capable of annihilating the opposition, had the other been absent. The result was an incredible battle between Bayliss and Edwards; in the first part of the season the former always had the upper hand, but at Laguna Seca the pendulum swung in favour of the American. Edwards' total regularity in terms of results, combined with the mishap that befell Bayliss with his crash at Assen, gave rise to a championship finale like no other. The two leading contenders for the title were in fact separated by one point on the eve of the race at Imola, where the excitement lasted right down to the final lap.

The pride of both riders prevented them from giving up one inch of track to the other in the sprint towards the chequered flag; in the last race in fact, Edwards did not even have to win to become world champion, but Bayliss could do nothing anyway to prevent the victory from going to the American. In any case they fought it out tooth and nail right from the start to the final heart-stopping lap. The best Spanish rider in the championship was Rubén Xaus, who in the last few races was the only rider capable of keeping on the pace of the champion and the runner-up, but his lack of a consistent run of results relegated him to sixth place.
Gregorio Lavilla, Juan Bautista Borja and, in the last two rounds, Jero Vidal did a decent job of completing the task that was required of them.

Ernest Ribé

A fter Imola, Superbike will never be the same again but Valentina is only 19 years old and she has no way of knowing. She was going to kindergarten when Fred Merkel wrote the first chapter of the legend. She could never have imagined that fifteen years later she would have left home before dawn for a two-hour journey that seemed like a never-ending adventure. When you dream about something for a long time, the reality sometimes does not live up to the imagination. When Valentina entered the paddock, Merkel had long gone. The former champion relives those moments of glory during his fishing trips to Lake Taupo in New Zealand. Now there are other heroes who pass by her in the paddock, ready for the challenge. She can get close enough to them to look them in the eyes. They are filled with determination, a will to win, total commitment. Valentina will also have eyes like that when her life requires it. When the race begins, she is glued to the metal fence, just a stone's throw away from the track. Captured by the excitement. She would love to be in a thousand different places at once, so as not to lose one single moment of the spectacle. An incredible excitement. Now that it's over, the race seems as if it had hardly lasted at all, and the seconds passed away as if in a dream. "If I had a child, I would have brought him here and he would have fallen in love with motorcycle racing".

Paolo Gozzi

13

The World Superbike Chanmpionship got underway in 1988 after its early years in the United States and Australia. In America in particular, many of the big names in Europe in the GP category passed through this four-stroke class: Wayne Rainey, AMA champion in 1983 and 1987, Fred Merkel, champion in 1984, 1985 and 1986, Kevin Schwantz and John Kocinski.

Nine rounds were organised in the first year, six in Europe and the others in Japan, Australia and New Zealand. The bikes were production-based with several important modifications, a rule aimed mainly at attracting large numbers of 'private' riders. The first World Superbike champion was American Fred Merkel who, on a Team Rumi Honda VFR, saw off the surprising challenge from ex-motocross rider Fabrizio Pirovano (Yamaha FZR).

GIANCARLO FALAPPA
BIMOTA - 1989

RAYMOND ROCHE – DUCATI - 1990

The two Bimota YB of Davide Tardozzi, the first-ever winner of a World Superbike race at Donington, and Stephane Mertens, as well as the Ducati 851 of Marco Lucchinelli, the first winner of a World Superbike round (Donington was decided on aggregate results), suffered numerous problems, which allowed the American to take the title. In this season, a certain Mick Doohan on a Yamaha won races at Sugo (Japan) and Oran Park (Australia).

In 1989 the calendar was increased to eleven rounds with the addition of a double-header in the USA and Canada. Despite the championship promoters going bankrupt, Superbike showed it had major potential and constantly attracted large crowds. Honda entered the scene with the RC30, a competitive version of its four-cylinder 750, with which Fred Merkel won a second world title, this time beating Stephane Mertens, who was also on a similar bike. The Ducati 851 showed considerable improvement over the previous year and in this season was raced by the expert and gutsy Frenchman Raymond Roche, together with Baldassare Monti. While Fabrizio Pirovano had another excellent season, the man to watch was Giancarlo Falappa, who won three races on a competitive Bimota.

1990 saw the arrival of the Flammini Group as promoters and they soon revived the category. A major contribution to this came with the victory of Ducati thanks to the superb performances of Roche, who won the championship from the two Honda riders Merkel and Mertens.

American Doug Polen, who was only scheduled by Ducati to take part in a few races and then to concentrate on the American series, dominated the opening round of the 1991 championship. Doug, riding a Fast by Ferracci Ducati, would instead go on to remain in the series, winning 17 out of the 26 races, including six double wins! Despite a superb second half of the season, Roche was unable to do anything against the American and settled for the runner-up slot. Stephane Mertens also went well now that he had switched to a Ducati, and so did Rob Phillis, who was turning the Kawasaki into force to be reckoned with.
Polen was still hungry for the wins

however and he repeated his triumph in 1992, taking a second successive title despite stiff opposition from Roche, who was determined to leave the series on a high note. The arrival of Kiwi Aaron Slight alongside Phillis in the Kawasaki team marked another step forward for the Japanese manufacturer, while Falappa (Ducati) and Pirovano (Yamaha) were also competitive.

The 1993 season saw the arrival of another American, Scott Russell. Thanks to the Muzzy team, the rider from Georgia had already taken part in a few WSBK races, but he was now involved full-time. The results were surprising to say the least and the rider with the redskin motif

DOUG POLEN – DUCATI – 1991

SCOTT RUSSELL – KAWASAKI - 1993

SUPERBIKE WINNERS

1988	FRED MERKEL	USA	HONDA
1989	FRED MERKEL	USA	HONDA
1990	RAYMOND ROCHE	F	DUCATI
1991	DOUG POLEN	USA	DUCATI
1992	DOUG POLEN	USA	DUCATI
1993	SCOTT RUSSELL	USA	KAWASAKI
1994	CARL FOGARTY	GB	DUCATI
1995	CARL FOGARTY	GB	DUCATI
1996	TROY CORSER	AUS	DUCATI
1997	JOHN KOCINSKI	USA	HONDA
1998	CARL FOGARTY	GB	DUCATI
1999	CARL FOGARTY	GB	DUCATI
2000	COLIN EDWARDS	USA	HONDA
2001	TROY BAYLISS	AUS	DUCATI
2002	COLIN EDWARDS	USA	HONDA

CARL FOGARTY – DUCATI – 1994

on his helmet took the world title from Giancarlo Falappa and Carl Fogarty on Ducatis. Slight finished third, followed by Pirovano in his last season on a Yamaha before moving to Ducati.

The following year Honda returned to WSBK in a big way with the splendid RC45, which was raced by the talented New Zealander Aaron Slight. The Castrol Honda rider was one of the stars of the 1994 season, battling against Carl Fogarty, who took the gorgeous Ducati 916 to its debut, and the outgoing champion Scott Russell. The American powered into an early championship lead, but from Spain onwards was then overhauled by Fogarty. Slight also had a brief spell at the top but his points in Britain were allowed and then taken away again due to a case of illegal fuel. The situation was complicated but Fogarty continued to aim for the title,

TROY CORSER – DUCATI – 1996

which he won with a text-book race at Phillip Island against Russell and Slight. No one could ever have imagined at the time that this would be the start of an incredible series of titles that 'Foggy' would go on to win for Ducati. The British rider repeated his triumph in 1995, the season in which the Italian manufacturer picked up its 100th WSBK win (in Austria), and which saw the emergence of the talented young Australian Troy Corser, winner of the AMA title.

The following year Fogarty decided to switch to Honda and in response Ducati signed none other than John Kocinski. The American joined the team run by Virginio Ferrari, who was one of the few people capable of managing the notoriously difficult American. Troy Corser was in a separately-run factory Ducati squad, while Fogarty's team-mate was Slight. These four riders were still in with a chance of taking the title as the season drew to a close, but the 1996 crown eventually went to the Australian after a double win at Albacete and a class performance on his home circuit.

World Superbike was shaken up again in 1997 when Fogarty and Kocinski swapped teams and Corser moved to GP racing, while Russell returned with Yamaha. Only Fogarty and Kocinski were in with a chance of winning however and in the end the title went to the American. Another of the stars of the season was Pierfrancesco Chili with a privately-run Ducati.

JOHN KOCINSKI HONDA - 1997

CARL FOGARTY – DUCATI - 1999

COLIN EDWARDS – HONDA - 2000

TROY BAYLISS – DUCATI - 2001

In 1998 the 23 year-old Japanese rider Noriyuki Haga burst onto the scene and, at least in the early rounds, proved to be tough opposition for Fogarty, who went on to conquer a third Riders' title. Unfortunately Haga crashed at Monza and the main opposition now became Colin Edwards, who was fast emerging for Castrol Honda after switching from Yamaha. Corser was also back on the pace, but it was Fogarty who finished the strongest after his difficult early part of the season. At the mid-point Aaron Slight also became a candidate for the title, but in the end he could only finish runner-up

as Fogarty took his third WSBK crown. Chili also had another good season with some superb performances on a Ducati. Carl Fogarty became the first rider to win four WSBK titles in 1999 on the Ducati 996. His domination was never in doubt and the British rider outdistanced second-placed men Colin Edwards (Honda) and Troy Corser (Ducati) by 130 points. Aaron Slight (Honda) and Akira Yanagawa (Kawasaki) also had good seasons.

The number of world championship victories for 'Foggy' could have been higher had it not been for a crash at the start of 2000 which first forced him to miss the rest of the season and then to retire from racing. It was tough blow for Superbike and for Ducati. The title went to Colin Edwards on the brand-new Honda VTR, five years after he had arrived in Superbike with Yamaha and three years after he had switched to Honda. Haga had looked to be favourite to win the title, but a rather murky question of doping ruined his season. Troy Bayliss exploded onto the scene after being drafted into Ducati from the AMA championship and the Australian surprisingly finished sixth overall. And still on the subject of Australians, Corser won some races in his debut season with Aprilia.

The 2001 season saw a new breed of hero emerge as Bayliss took the title, thanks also to a superbly competitive Ducati 998. His chief rival was again Edwards, who headed home his fellow-American Ben Bostrom (Ducati) in the championship standings. Corser failed to improve with the Aprilia, while Britain's Neil Hodgson had a positive season on a private Ducati.

SUPERBIKE
WORLD CHAMPIONSHIP
RACES

The 15th edition of the World Superbike Championship got underway at the Spanish circuit with reigning world champion Troy Bayliss starting from pole position, slightly quicker than team-mate Bostrom, Castrol Honda rider Colin Edwards and a returning Haga with the Aprilia. And it was the Japanese rider who looked as if he was going to be the biggest threat to the Ducati champion, twice finishing runner-up behind the irrepressible Troy. The gap from the winner was significant, but ten points between them gave out hope for the rest of the championship. Bayliss however was well on the way to repeating his 2001 exploits. American Ben Bostrom (Ducati-Dunlop) seemed as if he might offer some opposition after a terrific battle with Haga in race 1. After some excellent times in winter testing, Colin Edwards limited the damage with third and fourth place. The first four-cylinder challenger to the flag was the factory Kawasaki ZX-7RR in the hands of Japan's Izutsu, while the local riders failed to shine.

AUSTRALIAN ROUND
ISLAND, 22-23-24 MARCH 2002

Down on the other side of the world, in the second round of the championship, Colin Edwards was on top form, the American setting quickest time in qualifying, almost six-tenths of a second local hero and reigning champion Bayliss. Third was Haga, once again up at the front, ahead of Hodgson and Bostrom. The story was the same in the races however as Troy Bayliss scored another double win in front of 57,000 spectators to increase his championship lead. Behind was Colin Edwards, who had to settle for two second places, ahead of the other Ducati rider Ruben Xaus. Bostrom and Hodgson swapped places in the two races, while Haga (Aprilia) had an off-day with just a sixth place in race 2. The four-cylinder machines were well off the pace, Kawasaki's Izutsu again the best with sixth place in race 1, while Lavilla took the Suzuki to eighth place in race 2.

This time the gap was minimal but Texan Edwards again set pole in South Africa, ahead of Bayliss; third was Bostrom ahead of Haga and Hodgson (Ducati-HM). The warm-up saw a nasty crash for Pierfrancesco Chili, who made contact with Xaus and had to miss the South African round. 87,000 spectators watched in amazement as Troy Bayliss notched up his third double win of the season, increasing his points lead to 45 over Edwards, who finished second in race 1, more than four seconds away from the Australian, and third behind Xaus in race 2. Hodgson and Bostrom again exchanged positions and were already being left behind in the championship battle. Aprilia were even now further behind after an engine failure that forced Haga into retirement in race 1 after a spell in the lead, while in race 2 he finished sixth due to tyre problems. The token win amongst the four-cylinder machinery again went to Izutsu with the factory Kawasaki, with team-mate Walker right behind.

SUGO

As always, the presence of local `wild-card' riders provided a further element of interest in the Japanese round. And it was a rider from the Land of the Rising Sun who started from pole: no less than Noriyuki Haga, who powered to the front in qualifying, 17/1000ths (!) of a second ahead of Hodgson, the best Ducati rider. Third was 2001 winner Makoto Tamada with the Honda VTR 1000 SP, ahead of Bostrom, while Bayliss was only seventh on the grid. Qualifying also saw a nasty crash for Hitoyasu Izutsu, the best four-cylinder rider, putting him out of action for several months. Haga and his Aprilia were the stars of the two races, but the Japanese rider could only manage a third and fifth place after his tyres struggled to last the distance. Race 1 went to Edwards from Tamada, both on Hondas. Fourth was a lonely Hodgson, ahead of a struggling Bayliss and Yanagawa (Kawasaki). Tamada took revenge in race 2 after beating off opposition from Edwards and Hodgson, while Bayliss this time was fourth.

JAPAN

ITALY

W SBK returned to Europe for the first of three races in Italy and it was a surprise, after his early season results, to see Hodgson in pole position. The British Ducati satellite team rider was almost half-a-second quicker than Edwards and Bayliss! Fourth place in qualifying went to a returning Chili ahead of Haga. Monza also saw the return of the Benelli after the flyaway races, but the team still struggled in qualifying. In warm conditions, a massive 82,000 strong crowd cheered on the fourth double win of the season for Troy Bayliss and Ducati. In race 1 the Australian fought it out with Hodgson, Edwards and Chili, who finished in that order. In race 2 the world champion saluted the rest of the field and powered away to a lonely victory, leaving Edwards, Haga (Aprilia) and Hodgson to fight for second place, which went to the Texan. Lavilla took the singleton Suzuki to seventh and fifth places, while Ben Bostrom's brother Eric, in for Izutsu at Kawasaki, finished in a disappointing ninth place. The Benelli scored its first points of the 2002 season.

Superbike came to the British circuit for the first time and the race weekend saw a change of the rules to allow in four-cylinder 1000 cc bikes starting from 2003. Back to this year and it was Bayliss on pole with a superb lap in the last few minutes of a wet qualifying session. Behind was Colin Edwards, who had been on pole until the last few minutes, followed by Steve Hislop (Ducati) and Haga. Bayliss was the star of the two races: in the first he twice crashed in pouring rain, but got back up again to finish fifth. Edwards took the win after being the only rider to offer much opposition to the Australian cyclone (not for nothing was he nicknamed "tornado"). Behind the Texan, Haga finally finished on the podium ahead of local hero Hodgson. In race 2 Bayliss was faultless as he powered to his ninth win out of twelve races. Edwards easily held second place and reduced the points gap to 29 from Troy. Xaus completed the podium, while Chris Walker (Kawasaki) was a positive fourth. Goddard twice scored points for Benelli, but was some way off the front-runners.

UNITED KINGDOM ROUND
SILVERSTONE 24,25,26 MAY 2002

B ayliss was again on pole position for the first of the two German rounds; right behind was a reborn Ben Bostrom with the second Ducati and Edwards, followed by five more Ducatis. The superiority of the Italian bikes showed in the race, where the Australian went on to score another double win, allowing him to increase his lead over Edwards by a further ten points to 39. For his part the American tried to battle with Troy, but could only pick up two second places. Ruben Xaus completed the identical podiums with two thirds, ahead of Haga and Bostrom, who exchanged fourth and fifth in the two races. Pierfrancesco Chili twice finished sixth, results that allowed the Italian to catch up with the second group in the standings. Eighth and ninth went to the four-cylinder bikes, with Lavilla (Suzuki) in race 1 and Walker (Kawasaki) in race 2, while Benelli scored another championship point.

On a track he knows like the back of his hand, Troy Bayliss was in superb form, inflicting half-a-second on his closest rival Ben Bostrom in qualifying! The other riders were even further behind, in the order Edwards, Hodgson, youngster Toseland, Haga and an excellent Pedercini, one of the best Superbike privateers. After his performance in qualifying, it was not surprising to see Troy pick up another double win, and the Australian took his lead over Edwards to 49 points. The Honda-Castrol rider could do nothing but control his adversary and twice finished second. Neil Hodgson with a semi-factory Ducati was third and fourth, exchanging places with Noriyuki Haga (Aprilia); the two riders were also third and fourth in the championship standings, ahead of American Ben Bostrom who was twice fifth at Misano. Lavilla and Walker again shared the win amongst the four-cylinder brigade. All the talk at Misano was about the previous week's presentation of the Foggy Petronas and the testing being carried out by Mondial to bring the Piega into the world championship.

Colin Edwards, sporting a splendid stars and stripes livery on his Honda, was keen to score a good result at his home circuit and the Texan started the weekend in the best possible way by setting pole in qualifying ahead of an increasingly on-form Hodgson, Bayliss and Haga. Behind came two American riders: Eric Bostrom (Kawasaki) and Yates (Suzuki). In race 1 the real star was Haga with the Aprilia, who put in a superb recovery only to finish in the gravel. Bayliss took the win again in a sprint finish to the line with team-mate Ruben Xaus; Edwards was third, followed by the talented 21-year-old American Nicky Hayden. Castrol Honda's Texan rider however dominated race 2 with a superb performance ahead of Bayliss and Hodgson in second and third. Eric Bostrom won the battle with his brother by beating him to the line. A good performance also came from Toseland (Ducati), Haga had a disappointing second race, while the Benelli continued to notch up the points.

The second British round was another thriller, with Troy Bayliss crashing out in qualifying and fracturing a rib after making contact with team-mate Xaus. This did not prevent the tough Australian from taking part in Superpole however, where he set fourth quickest time that enabled him to start from the front row of the grid together with Hodgson, Edwards and Rutter (Ducati). Chili, always on top form at Brands Hatch, was fifth quickest. Bayliss was certainly not in the best of condition, especially on a tough circuit like Brands and had to settle for a third and a second place in the two races, which were won by Colin Edwards in front of more than 120,000 spectators. The American had now reduced Troy's lead to 39 points, while in race 2 Hodgson let Bayliss pass to limit the damage. Haga was struggling with the Aprilia but picked up a fourth and fifth place. Chris Walker on a Kawasaki was the best of the four-cylinder brigade with a sixth and eighth place on his home circuit, while the Foggy Petronas FP1 did a couple of demonstration laps with Corser and Haydon on board.

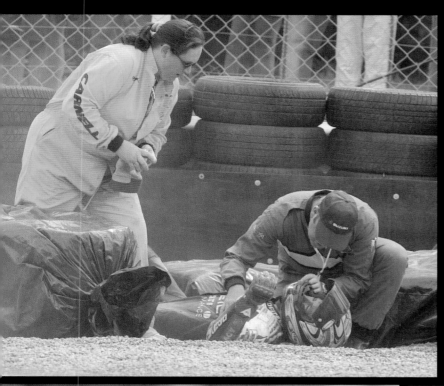

The final part of the season got underway at the German circuit, where British rider Neil Hodgson set pole, ahead of Edwards, who now had a revised VTR SPW, and Bostrom.

Bayliss was only sixth on the grid after failing to get the best possible set-up for the race.

Colin Edwards then powered to victory ahead of Bayliss and Hodgson, who will replace the Australian as Ducati factory rider in 2003. Race 2 saw exactly the same podium, with Haga (Aprilia) fourth after challenging Hodgson in the last few laps.

Edwards was now 29 points away from Bayliss, who was coming under increasing pressure from the Texan.

Gregorio Lavilla was the quickest four-cylinder rider to the flag on an Alstare-Suzuki, while both Chili and Bostrom had good races.

GERMANY

Get Well Soon COLIN ! (But Not Too Soon !!)

SUPERBIKE

Qualifying was almost a carbon copy of the Oschersleben race, with Colin Edwards on pole, one-tenth of a second ahead of Xaus and a nervous Bayliss, who had crashed during practice. To underline the Texan's performance, his time was just 54/1000ths of a second slower than Valentino Rossi's in June's Dutch Grand Prix. Colin was on top form in the race as well, picking up the double win that allowed him to take over from Bayliss in the standings by one point. The Australian finished runner-up in race 1 but then crashed out from third place in the second race, incredibly losing the lead he had held since the start of the championship. Nori Haga (Aprilia) also put in a good race with a podium and Pierfrancesco Chili was a superb second in race 2 ahead of a rapidly-improving Toseland. Lavilla (Suzuki) and Walker (Kawasaki) won the two four-cylinder races, while the Benelli again finished in the points.

The tension could be cut with a knife as the teams arrived at the legendary Imola circuit for the final round. Colin Edwards immediately laid his cards on the table with some incredible times throughout the practice sessions. It goes without saying that he started from pole position, while his title rival Bayliss was third behind team-mate Xaus. It was clear however that the battle was going to be between the two champions. Edwards powered into the lead and stayed there until the race was stopped for oil on the track. Bayliss responded and picked up the win in the second part but the American was first on aggregate times. Third was Ruben Xaus, who had tried in vain to catch the leading duo to give a hand to Troy. Colin and Troy then put on a fantastic show for the almost 100,000 spectators at the Santerno circuit in race 2. The Texan blasted into the lead, but Bayliss counterattacked with some superb passing moves. In the end the win went to the Honda rider, one second ahead of Bayliss, but the title belonged to Edwards. The end of the race is a triumph that sees the two protagonists of the 2002 season together on the podium.

SUPERBIKE
WORLD CHAMPIONSHIP
RIDERS

Colin Edwards

There is one thing about Edwards that is particularly fascinating: his determination. Even when everything seems to be lost, he continues to fight on with the same determination as before; it was this total commitment that enabled the 'Texas Tornado' to win his second World Superbike title in 2002.

The rider who succeeded in defeating Troy Bayliss to win the crown is a changed man. The duel between Edwards and

Bayliss went right down to the wire at Imola and on that occasion Colin managed to control the situation, not only by focussing his race on Bayliss, but also by his determination to win in front of all the Italian fans who applauded his well-deserved victory.

He controlled the situation throughout the championship, even at Laguna when he was 50 points behind the Ducati rider, a lead that seemed totally out of reach given the ability of his Australian opponent. Nevertheless from Laguna race 2 onwards, Colin scored nine successive wins to take the world championship at the final round.

Colin Edwards

Colin Edwards II was born on February 27, 1974 in Houston (Texas); he made his racing debut in 1991, winning his first professional race the following year on the prestigious Daytona track. He first took part in the WSBK championship in 1995 on a Yamaha, finishing 11th overall in his first season and fifth the following year. After a disappointing 1997, Colin started his climb to the top by switching to Honda: with three wins he finished fifth overall, and then became championship runner-up the following year.

Colin Edwards

2000 was the year the Honda VTR arrived and Colin seized the opportunity by winning the title. The rest is history and it also includes his wins in the prestigious Suzuka 8 Hours race in Japan.

What about his numerous records? Colin Edwards is the rider who has scored the most successive podium finishes in a season (25), who won the most successive races (nine), and who gave the 100th WSBK win to the USA and the 50th to Honda.

A keen golfer, snowboarder and motocross rider, the Texan lives in Conroe with his wife Alyssia.

SUPERBIKE

The Honda VTR had already made a name for itself on its debut in 2000 when it won the WSBK championship with Colin Edwards. Now the VTR 1000 SP-2 has picked up a second world title in three years. It was the Japanese manufacturer's response to Ducati, which it had tried to beat for many years with the RC30 and the RC45. Honda simply decided to play on the same terrain as the Bologna manufacturer, by producing a twin-cylinder bike, which won the Riders' title in 2000, finished second in 2001 and first again this year. The bike was exclusively given to Edwards, while other versions were raced by American and Japanese teams. There was a also a 'customer' bike given to Team Rumi for British rider Mark Heckles in the World Superbike Championship.

58

Mark Heckles

Engine

Type: 90° V-twin
Capacity: 999 cc
Bore and stroke: 100 x 63.6 mm
Valves: four per cylinder
Brake Horse Power: 175 HP at 12,000 rpm

Cycle part

Frame: Aluminium twin spar
Front suspension: Showa 47 mm upside down forks
Rear suspension: Showa fully adjustable unit

Transmission

Gearbox: Six-speed with adjustable ratios
Clutch: Wet multiple plate with slipper device

Brakes

Make: Nissin
Front: dual 320 mm discs with 6-piston calipers, floating stainless steel discs
Rear: single 220 mm disc with single-piston caliper

Tyres

Make: Michelin
Front: 120/60 - 16,5 "
Rear: 180/60 - 16,5"

Dimension

Length: n.d.
Width: n.d.
Dry weight: 164 Kg
Wheelbase: 1.424 mm

Troy Bayliss

Many words have been written about this Australian rider, who burst onto the world scene due to unexpected circumstances (Fogarty's crash in 2000), and who immediately attracted the attention of experts and fans alike. Born on March 30, 1969 in Taree, Troy started racing in 1992, and made his WSBK debut in 1997 as a wild-card in his home race (twice finishing fifth on a Suzuki). He was then racing for the Ducati team in the AMA championship when he was called on to replace Fogarty. Immediately the Superbike circus was bowled over by this rider, who is always affable towards the fans and who is always accompanied by his wife Kim and often his two children Mitchell and Abbey.

Troy Bayliss

When he is on the bike, Troy is a lot less sociable towards others, despite being very correct out on the track: out of 76 races in which he has taken part, Troy has won 22, finishing sixth in 2000, taking the world title in 2001 and runner-up slot in 2002.

In 2002 he had a fantastic first half of the season with 14 wins in 18 races! Then a couple of crashes must have led to a slight loss in concentration and despite some incredible races in considerable pain, the return of Colin Edwards meant that he was unable to clinch a second successive world title.

His duel with the American at Imola will go down in the history of motorcycle racing, not only Superbike, and relinquishing the # 1 plate at that fantastic circuit in front of 100,000 spectators was an honourable way to go.

DUCATI 998 R factory

What more can be said about the most successful twin-cylinder bike in the WSBK championship? Very little actually, except for the fact that the 998 Factory '02 with "Testastretta" engine is the most recent version of the celebrated bike which has won 11 world constructors' titles, including one in 2002, since its debut in the category. And the series shows no sign of ending.

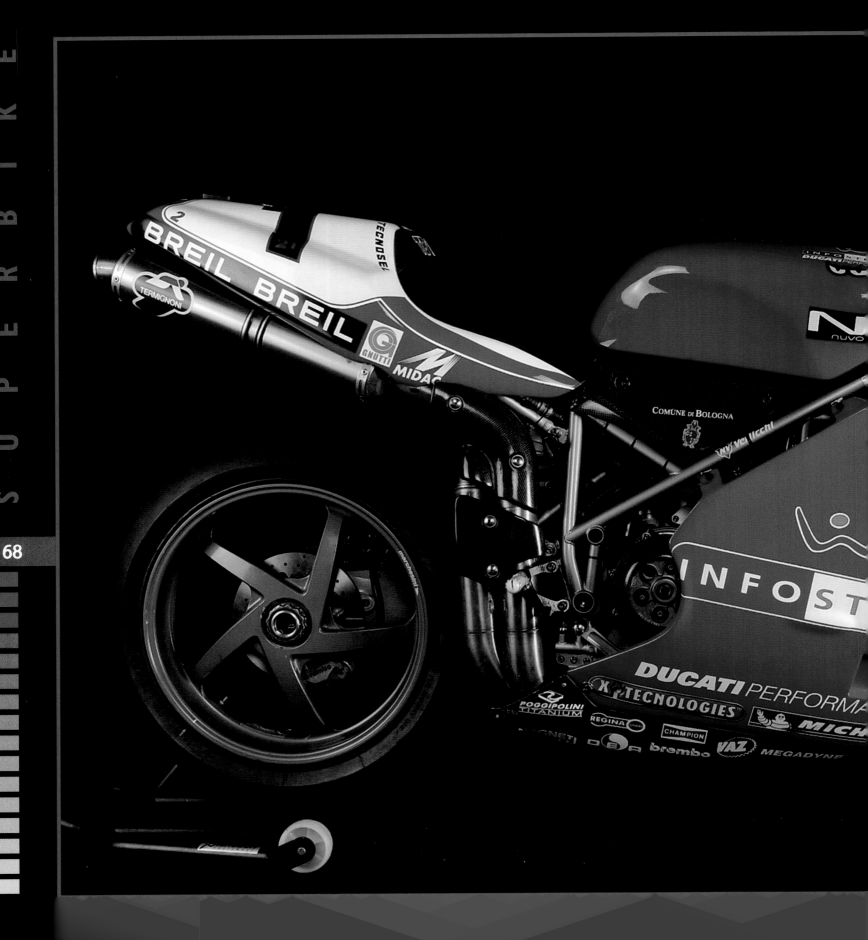

Engine
Type: L 90° twin-cylinder 'Testastretta'
Capacity: 999 cc
Bore and stroke: 104 x 58.8 mm
Valves: four per cylinder
Carburation: two single-injector throttle bodies
Crankshaft horsepower: 188 HP at 12,500 rpm

Cycle part
Frame: tubular steel trestle
Front suspension: 42 mm upside-down Ohlins fork
Rear suspension: single-sided magnesium swingarm, with Ohlins shock-absorber

Transmission
Gearbox: six-speed
Clutch: dry multiplate

Brakes
Make: Brembo
Front: dual 290 or 320 mm floating discs
Rear: single 200 mm or vented 218 mm floating disc

Tyres
Make: Michelin or Dunlop
Front: 12/60 16,5"
Rear: 19/67 16,5"

Dimension
Length: 2,045 mm
Width: 680 mm
Dry weight: 164 kg with oil and water
Wheelbase: 1,425 mm
Fuel tank: 23.9 l t

Neil Hodgson
Jamie Toseland

Britain once again has top-quality riders to count on. These surely include the two riders of the HM Plant Ducati team (GSE), who had outstanding seasons. Hodgson, born in Burnley in 1973 was once again back on a competitive bike (the ex-works 998 Testatretta), and finished an excellent third overall in the world championship, picking up two seconds and numerous podiums.

For his part 22-year-old Toseland (from Sheffield) was taking part in his second WSBK season and finished seventh overall with a series of performances that catapulted him to the attention of experts as one of the most promising young riders in this category.

Even though their positions in the championship can certainly not be considered as negative (the American was fifth and the Spaniard sixth), both factory Ducati riders had a disappointing season. Ben was unable to repeat his exploits of the previous season, maybe due to the limits of his Dunlop tyres, while Ruben was top 3 material but despite some spectacular riding was also disappointing.

Bostrom, born in 1974 in Redding (California), scored his best result and only podium finish at Valencia with third place, while the 24 year-old Xaus from Barcelona twice finished second behind Bayliss at Kyalami and Laguna Seca.

RIDERS

APRILIA RSV 1000

Engine
Type: Doch V60° twin-cylinder
Capacity: 1000 cc
Bore and stroke: 100x63.4 mm
Valves: four per cylinder
Crankshaft power: over 170 HP

Cycle part
Frame: Aprilia aluminium twin beam
Front suspension: Ohlins upside-down fork
Rear suspension: Ohlins single shock with progressive link

Transmission
Gearbox: six-speed
Clutch system: Multi-disc dry clutch with reverse torque control

Brakes
Make: Brembo
Front: dual 320 mm floating discs
Rear: single 218 mm floating disc

Tyres
Make: Dunlop
Front: 120/60 17" or 120/75 16.5"
Rear: 190/55 17" or 195-200/60 16.5"

Dimension
Length: 2,030 mm
Width: 700 mm
Dry weight: 164 Kg
Wheel base: 1,410/1,415 mm
Fuel tank: capacity 24 Lt

Noriyuki Haga

A lot was expected of Haga on his return to the WSBK championship and the spectacular rider from Aichi (Japan) failed to disappoint with some fantastic performances that earned him the plaudits from fans everywhere once again. 27 years old, with 11 wins to his name, Nory is one of the most popular riders in Superbike and now even Aprilia is becoming increasingly popular amongst fans and experts alike. In 2002 this extraordinary pairing finished in fourth place and Haga was on the podium seven times.

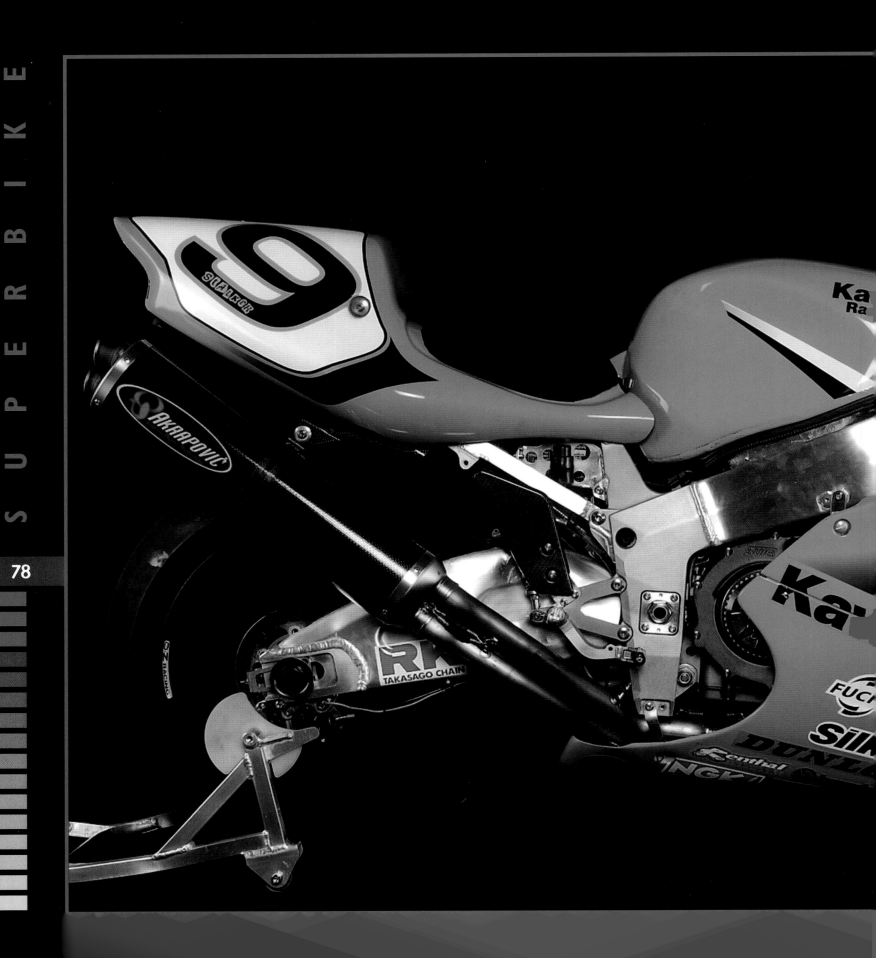

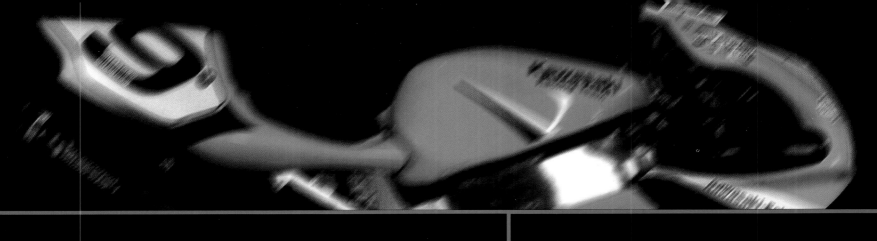

Engine
Type: liquid-cooled, in-line four-cylinders
Capacity: 749 cc
Bore and stroke: 73 x 44.7 mm
Valves: four per cylinder
Crankshaft horsepower: 158 HP at 13,800 rpm

Cycle part
Front suspension: Ohlins upside-down fork
Rear suspension: Ohlins single shock-absorber

Transmission
Gearbox: six-speed with adjustable ratios
Clutch: dry

Brakes
Make: Brembo
Front: dual 320 mm discs
Rear: single Nissin disc

Tyres
Make: Dunlop
Front: 120/75 17"
Rear: 195/55 16,5"

Dimension
Length: n.d.
Width: n.d.
Dry weight: 162 kg
Wheelbase: 1,435 mm
Fuel tank: capacity 24 Lt

Chris Walker
Hitoyasu Izutsu
Eric Bostrom

Kawasaki, heavily involved in MotoGP development, once again lined up with the ZX-7RR 750, but it really only raced for the symbolic four-cylinder title. As well as the two riders for the Harald-Eckl-run factory squad, American Eric Bostrom also rode the 'green machine', replacing the injured Izutsu for several races. The best result for the team was fourth place for Walker at Silverstone and Bostrom at Laguna Seca. The 30 year-old British rider finished highest in the standings, ninth overall.

SUZUKI GSX-R 750

Engine
Type: Four cylinders in-line
Capacity: 749 cc
Bore and stroke: 72.0 x 46.0 mm
Horsepower: n.d.

Cycle part
Frame: Twin-spar (aluminium alloy)
Front suspension: Inverted telescopic, coil
spring, spring pre-load fully adjustable,
rebound damping force fully adjustable
Rear suspension: Link type, oil damped,
coil spring, spring pre-load fully adjustable,
rebound damping force and compression
damping force fully adjustable

Transmission
Gearbox: 6-speed, constant mesh
Clutch: dry

Brakes
Make: Tokico
Front: 4-piston calipers, dual disc
Rear: 2-piston calipers, single disc

Tyres
Make: Dunlop
Front: 120/70ZR 17"
Rear: 180/55ZR 17"

Dimension
Length: 2.040 mm
Width: 715 mm
Dry weight: 166 kg
Wheelbase: 1.410 mm
Fuel tank: capacity 18.0 Lt

Gregorio Lavilla

One of the riders with the most WSBK races to his name, Gregorio had an up-and-down season after struggling with an uncompetitive 750 Suzuki against the 100cc twins. Despite the efforts of Team Suzuki Alstare Corona Extra, the gap could not be bridged and 29 year-old Gregorio from Tarragona was left with little but to fight for the token win in the four-cylinder class. In the end he finished tenth overall, while his best result was a sixth place in Misano race 2.

Engine
Type: inline 3 cylinder; inclined forward 15°
Capacity: 898 cc
Bore and stroke: 88 x 49.2 mm
Valves: four per cylinder
Crankshaft horsepower: more than 170 HP at 13.000 rpm

Cycle part
Frame: front section in chrommolybdenum steel tubes; rear section in aluminium alloy
Front suspension: upside-down fork fully adjustable
Rear suspension: pressed aluminium swingarm with monoshock

Transmission
Gearbox: six-speed, entirely removable
Clutch: dry clutch with anti-blocking system

Brakes
Make: Brembo
Front: double 290-305-320 mm floating discs with 4 pistons radials calipers
Rear: single 160 mm disc with 2 pistons caliper

Tyres
Make: Dunlop
Front: 120/70 16,5"
Rear: 195/60 16,5"

Dimension
Length: 2,060 mm
Width: 704 mm
Dry weight: 162 kg
Wheelbase: 1,420-1,440 mm
Fuel tank: capacity 24 Lt

Peter Goddard

A change in the engineering staff was not enough to improve the competitiveness of the original three-cylinder Italian bike. The 37 year-old Australian Goddard gave 100% as always but despite his efforts the team only picked up 23 points. The best result was 11th place at Assen, which failed to compensate for the efforts of this interesting project.

Pierfrancesco Chili

Broc Parkes

Juan Bautista Borja

PIERFRANCESCO CHILI

"Frankie" continues to be one of the stars of the championship. At the ripe old age of 37, the Bologna rider raced with a Ducati for team NCR-Axo-Poggipolini. His best result in 2002 was a splendid second place at Assen, which crowned an excellent second half of the season. Chili, one of the 'veterans' of Superbike, has 15 wins to his name.

BROC PARKES

The 20 year-old Australian raced with a Parmalat-sponsored NCR Ducati in 2002, finishing 11th overall in the championship standings. His best results in his second WSBK season were three eighth places.

JUAN BAUTISTA BORJA

In his eleventh season of racing and third in Superbike, the 32 year-old from Altea (Spain) finished 12th overall in the championship on a Team Spaziotel Ducati. His best performance was seventh at Silverstone.

Lucio Pedercini
Marco Borciani
Serafino Foti

All three riders raced for a competitive, 'family-run' team. Lucio (born 29 years ago in Volta Mantovana) was the best of the three with 13th overall (best result was sixth at Monza). 26 year-old Marco from Desenzano sul Garda (Brescia) continued his experience with the twin-cylinder bike from Bologna, finishing 15th overall; for his part 34 year-old Serafino, from Turin, returned on a regular basis to WSBK and finished in the points seven times, in 25th position overall.

Alessandro Antonello
Steve Martin

The DFX team was selected by Pirelli to test its Superbike tyres in the hands of Australian Steve Martin and Italian Alessandro Antonello, in his first full SBK season. They finished 16th and 20th respectively. Martin was born in Chastone in 1968, while Antonello, ex-test rider for Aprilia, comes from Citadella (Padova) and was born in 1972.

Mauro Sanchini
Ivan Clementi

Sergio Bertocchi, the owner of the team of the same name which races with Kawasakis, chose an unusual pairing for their first experience with four-cylinder machines. 32 year-old Mauro from Monte Calvo in Foglia (Urbino) was taking part in his third year in SBK, while Ivan, born in 1975 in Montegiorgio (Ascoli Piceno) was making his debut in the category. 'Super Sanchio' finished in nineteenth place, while his team-mate was 31st overall.

Takeshi Tsujimura
Akira Yanagawa
Makoto Tamada

Every round of the World Superbike Championship saw the participation of several 'wild-card' riders who compete in their own national championship and are granted a place in their home round of the world series. The strongest riders are usually the Japanese, who always go well at Sugo. In particular Tamada, factory Honda rider, won race 2 at Sugo, while Yanagawa (Kawasaki) and Tsujimura (Yamaha) settled respectively for two sixth places and two tenths.

99

Aaron Yates
Nicky Hayden
Mathew Mladin

The Laguna Seca track is particularly testing and the Americans give their everything to outpace and beat the WSBK regulars on their home turf. This year, as well as Eric Bostrom and Doug Chandler, three more stars of the AMA Championship also had entries at the Californian round: 30 year-old Mladin and 28 year-old Yates with Yoshimura Suzukis and 20 year-old phenomenon Nicky Hayden with an American Honda. Hayden was the best of the bunch, finishing fourth in race 1.

Shane Byrne
Michael Rutter

Several BSB regulars also took part in the two British rounds, including Shane Byrne and Michael Rutter, who put up a good showing against their WSBK colleagues. They both rode Renegade Ducati 998s.

RIDERS

SUPERBIKE

First Line: Championship Standings - Second Line: Ranking Progression

For each rider the first row shows Championship Standings (points) and the second row shows Ranking Progression. Each event has two races (R1 / R2).

# Rider	Points	Pts From First	Pts From Prev	SPAIN Mar10 R1	R2	AUSTRALIA Mar24 R1	R2	S.AFRICA Apr7 R1	R2	JAPAN Apr21 R1	R2	ITALY1 May12 R1	R2	GT BRITAIN May26 R1	R2	GERMANY1 Jun9 R1	R2	S.MARINO Jun23 R1	R2	USA Jul14 R1	R2	EUROPE Jul28 R1	R2	GERMANY2 Sep1 R1	R2	NETHER. Sep8 R1	R2	ITALY2 Sep29 R1	R2
1 EDWARDS	552			13	16	20	20	20	16	25	20	16	20	25	20	20	20	20	20	16	25	25	25	25	25	25	25	25	25
				4	3	2	2	2	2	2	2	2	2	2	2	2	2	2	2	2	2	2	2	2	2	2	1	1	1
2 BAYLISS	541	11		25	25	25	25	25	25	11	13	25	25	11	25	25	25	25	25	25	20	16	20	20	20	20		20	20
				1	1	1	1	1	1	1	1	1	1	1	1	1	1	1	1	1	1	1	1	1	1	1	2	2	2
3 HODGSON	326	226	215	10	11	11	13	11	13	13	16	20	13	16	10	8		16	13	11	16	20	16	16	16	13		13	11
				6	5	5	5	5	5	4	3	3	3	3	3	3	3	3	3	3	3	3	3	3	3	3	3	3	3
4 HAGA	278	274	48	20	20	10		10		16	11	16		20	6	13	11	13	16			13	11	9	13	16	10	11	13
				2	2	4	4	6	6	6	5	6	4	4	4	4	4	4	4	4	5	4	4	5	5	4	4	4	4
5 B. BOSTROM	261	291	17	16	13	13	11	13	11	9	9	7		9	8	11	13	11	11	8	11	9	13	13	10	8	11	6	7
				3	3	3	3	3	4	3	4	5	5	5	6	6	6	5	5	5	4	5	4	4	4	5	5	5	5
6 XAUS	249	303	12	11		16	16	16	20	7		10		8	16	16	16			20		11	10	11		13		16	16
				5	9	7	6	4	3	5	6	4	6	6	5	5	5	6	6	6	6	6	6	6	6	6	6	6	6
7 TOSELAND	195	357	54	4	6	8	9	10	8	7	5	11		6	7	9	9	8		7	10	7		10	8	10	16	10	10
				12	10	9	9	8	8	7	7	7	7	7	7	7	7	7	7	7	7	7	7	7	7	7	7	7	7
8 CHILI	167	385	28	7								13		13	5	10	10	10	9	4	9	8	9	11	9	11	20	9	
				9	12	15	16	18	18	21	22	13	16	13	13	11	10	10	10	10	9	9	9	9	9	8	8	8	8
9 WALKER	152	400	15	6	9	7	7	8	7	5	3	6		2	13	7		9	8	5	6	10	8	7	1	9		5	4
				10	7	8	7	8	9	8	8	8	8	8	8	8	8	8	8	8	8	8	8	8	8	9	9	9	9
10 LAVILLA	130	422	22	8		9	8	5		4	4	9	11	2		8		6	10			1	4	8	7	9		8	9
				8	11	10	10	11	11	11	12	9	9	9	9	9	9	9	9	9	10	10	10	10	10	10	10	10	10
11 PARKES	77	475	53	1		3		5	2			8		4		5		2		1	4			6	6	7	8	7	8
				15	19	20	18	16	14	15	18	23	18	18	16	15	16	17	17	18	18	18	18	17	15	14	13	11	11
12 BORJA	74	478	3	5	8	4	6	7	6	2	1	5		9								5	5			6		5	
				11	8	10	11	10	10	10	11	12	12	12	10	10	11	11	11	11	11	11	11	11	11	11	11	12	12
13 PEDERCINI	71	481	3	2	5	6		4				10				6	6	7	7					3	4	6		2	3
				14	12	12	12	13	13	14	15	17	13	14	14	14	14	13	11	11	11	12	12	12	12	12	12	13	13
14 IZUTSU	62	490	9	9	10	10		9	9											3		5						1	6
				7	6	6	7	7	7	9	9	9	10	10	11	12	12	12	13	13	14	13	13	13	13	14	14	14	14
15 BORCIANI	55	497	7			4	5	6	3							4	4	5	6			1		5	5	5	7		
				15		14	15	12	12	13	14	15	19	19	20	19	17	16	16	16	17	17	17	18	18	16	14	15	15
16 MARTIN	52	500	3	7		3						6	5			7	5	3	4	2	5							3	2
				12		13	13	14	15	16	19	18	14	16	17	15	15	15	15	15	14	15	15	15	15	17	17	16	16
17 E. BOSTROM	49	503	3							3	2	7	9	5						10	13								
										25	24	21	14	15	15	17	17	18	19	17	13	14	14	14	14	14	14	17	17
18 TAMADA	45	507	4							20	25																		
										12	10	11	11	11	12	13	13	14	14	14	16	16	16	16	17	18	18	18	18
19 SANCHINI	41	511	4	1		1	4	3				4	3	1		2	2	4	5	1				2		3	4	1	
				19		18	17	16	17	19	21	20	21	21	22	21	20	19	17	19	19	19	19	19	19	19	19	19	19
20 ANTONELLO	38	514	3	3		2	5					8		3		3						4	3			3		4	
				13	16	16	13	14	15	16	19	15	19	19	17	18	19	20	20	20	20	20	19	19	20	20	20	20	20
21 BYRNE	30	522	8											7	11							6	6						
														26	20	22	22	22	22	22	22	21	21	21	21	21	21	21	21
22 GODDARD	23	529	7									2		3	1	1		1		2				4		4	5		
												28	28	28	27	27	27	27	27	29	29	29	30	27	27	23	22	22	22
23 YANAGAWA	20	532	3							10	10																		
										16	13	13	16	17	19	20	21	21	21	21	21	22	22	22	22	22	23	23	23
24 YATES	17	535	3																	9	8								
																				28	23	23	23	23	23	24	24	24	24
25 FOTI	17	535	0	2				4	1			4								2				2		2			
				18		18	20	19	18	21	22	24	24	25	26	26	26	24	24	24	26	26	26	24	24	24	24	24	24
26 HAYDEN	16	536	1																	13	3								
																				24	24	24	24	24	24	26	26	26	26
27 YOSHIKAWA	16	536	0							8	8																		
										20	16	18	21	22	23	23	23	23	23	23	24	24	24	24	24	26	26	26	26
28 HECKLES	15	537	1			2						1		10												1		1	
						20		21	21	26	26	26	27	23	24	24	24	24	24	24	24	24	26	26	26	27	27	28	28

R I D E R S

Pos	Rider	Points	Points From First	Points From Previous	March 10 SPAIN	March 24 AUSTRALIA	April 7 SOUTH AFRICA	April 21 JAPAN	May 12 ITALY 1	May 26 GREAT BRITAIN	June 9 GERMANY 1	June 23 SAN MARINO	July 14 UNITED STATES	July 28 EUROPE	September 1 GERMANY 2	September 8 NETHERLANDS	September 29 ITALY 2
29	TSUJIMURA	12	540	3				6 6 / 23 17	21 23	24 25	25 25	26 26	27 28	28 28	29 29	29 29	29 29
30	RUTTER	11	541	1						4 / 29 29	29 29	29 29	32 33	7 / 33 29	30 30	30 30	30 30
31	CLEMENTI	11	541	0	3 / 16	1 / 17 18	20 20	24 25	2 / 25 25	27 27	27 28	28 28	30 31	31 32	32 32	3 / 32 30	2 / 30 30
32	CHANDLER	10	542	1									3 7 / 35 29	29 30	31 31	31 32	32 32
33	MLADIN	6	546	4									6 / 30 31	31 32	32 33	33 33	33 33
34	HOFMANN	4	548	2							1 3 / 32 29	29 29	32 33	33 34	34 34	34 34	34 34
35	VALIA	4	548	0					3 1 / 26 26	29 29	29 29	29 29	32 33	33 34	34 34	34 34	34 34
36	MALATESTA	3	549	1								3 / 32	35 36	36 36	36 36	36 36	36 36
37	STEY	3	549	0		2 / 21 21	26 26	28 28	31 31	31 32	32 32	1 / 32 32	35 36	36 36	36 36	36 36	36 36
38	RICHARDS	2	550	1										2 / 38	38 38	38 38	38 38
39	ELLISON	2	550	0										2 / 38 38	38 38	38 38	38 38
40	VIDAL	1	551	1												1 / 40 40	40 40
41	TAKEDA	1	551	0				1 / 28 28	30 30	32 32	32 33	33 34	38 38	39 40	40 40	40 40	40 40

First Line: Championship Standings - Second Line: Ranking Progression

M A N U F A C T U R E S

Pos	Manufacturer	Points	Points From First	Points From Previous	March 10 SPAIN	March 24 AUSTRALIA	April 7 SOUTH AFRICA	April 21 JAPAN	May 12 ITALY 1	May 26 GREAT BRITAIN	June 9 GERMANY 1	June 23 SAN MARINO	July 14 UNITED STATES	July 28 EUROPE	September 1 GERMANY 2	September 8 NETHERLANDS	September 29 ITALY 2
1	DUCATI	575	·		25 25 / 1 1	25 25 / 1 1	25 25 / 1 1	13 16 / 1 1	25 25 / 1 1	16 25 / 1 1	25 25 / 1 1	25 25 / 1 1	25 20 / 1 1	20 20 / 1 1	20 20 / 1 1	20 20 / 1 1	20 20 / 1 1
2	HONDA	557	18		13 16 / 3 3	20 20 / 2 2	20 16 / 2 2	25 25 / 2 2	16 20 / 2 2	25 20 / 2 2	20 20 / 2 2	20 20 / 2 2	16 25 / 2 2	25 25 / 2 2	25 25 / 2 2	25 25 / 2 2	25 25 / 2 2
3	APRILIA	278	297	279	20 20 / 2 2	10 / 3 3	10 / 3 3	16 11 / 3 3	16 / 3 3	20 6 / 3 3	13 11 / 3 3	13 16 / 3 3	3	13 11 / 3 3	9 13 / 3 3	16 10 / 3 3	11 13 / 3 3
4	KAWASAKI	208	367	70	9 10 / 4 4	10 7 / 4 4	9 9 / 4 4	10 10 / 4 4	7 9 / 4 4	5 13 / 4 4	2 7 / 4 4	9 8 / 4 4	10 13 / 4 4	10 8 / 4 4	7 3 / 4 4	3 9 / 4 4	5 6 / 4 4
5	SUZUKI	147	428	61	8 / 5 5	9 8 / 5 5	5 / 5 5	4 4 / 5 5	9 11 / 5 5	2 / 5 5	8 / 5 5	6 10 / 5 5	9 8 / 5 5	1 4 / 5 5	8 7 / 5 5	9 / 5 5	8 9 / 5 5
6	BENELLI	23	552	124						2 / 7 7	3 1 / 7 7	1 / 7 7	1 / 7 7	2 / 7 7	4 / 7 7	4 5 / 6 6	6 6
7	YAMAHA	16	559	7				8 8 / 6 6	6 6	6 6	6 6	6 6	6 6	6 6	6 6	7 7	7 7

First Line: Championship Standings - Second Line: Ranking Progression

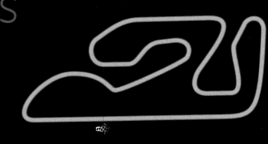

VALENCIA - ESP

8-9-10 March, 2002

RACE 1

Laps 23 = 92,115 km - Avg. 149,918 km/h

	No.	Rider	Nat	Team	Bike	Laps	Time	Gap	Speed	Fastest Lap
1	1	T. BAYLISS	AUS	Ducati Infostrada	Ducati 998 F 02	23	36'51.963		278,1	7 1'35.639
2	41	N. HAGA	JPN	Playstation2-FGF Aprilia	Aprilia RSV 1000	23	36'55.139	3.176	284,0	6 1'35.701
3	155	B. BOSTROM	USA	Ducati L & M	Ducati 998 F 02	23	36'55.279	3.316	283,3	5 1'35.677
4	2	C. EDWARDS	USA	Castrol Honda	Honda VTR 1000 SP2	23	36'55.990	4.027	281,8	5 1'35.721
5	11	R. XAUS	ESP	Ducati Infostrada	Ducati 998 F 02	23	37'00.673	8.710	281,8	4 1'35.910
6	100	N. HODGSON	GBR	HM Plant Ducati	Ducati 998 F 01	23	37'06.408	14.445	278,1	4 1'35.929
7	14	H. IZUTSU	JPN	Kawasaki Racing	Kawasaki ZX-7RR	23	37'07.858	15.895	284,0	4 1'36.181
8	10	G. LAVILLA	ESP	Alstare Suzuki Corona	Suzuki GSX-R750 Y	23	37'22.778	30.815	280,3	6 1'36.341
9	7	P. CHILI	ITA	Ducati NCR	Ducati 998 RS	23	37'22.783	30.820	278,1	4 1'36.165
10	9	C. WALKER	GBR	Kawasaki Racing	Kawasaki ZX-7RR	23	37'23.559	31.596	275,3	4 1'36.561
11	33	J. BORJA	ESP	Spaziotel Racing	Ducati 998 RS	23	37'23.630	31.667	281,8	7 1'36.753
12	52	J. TOSELAND	GBR	HM Plant Ducati	Ducati 998 F 01	23	37'28.233	36.270	278,9	7 1'37.030
13	30	A. ANTONELLO	ITA	DFX Racing Ducati Pirelli	Ducati 998 RS	23	37'31.935	39.972	284,8	5 1'36.745
14	19	L. PEDERCINI	ITA	Pedercini	Ducati 998 RS	23	37'35.765	43.802	274,6	8 1'37.156
15	12	B. PARKES	AUS	Ducati NCR	Ducati 996 R	23	37'38.615	46.652	278,9	11 1'37.285
16	20	M. BORCIANI	ITA	Pedercini	Ducati 998 RS	23	37'39.535	47.572	279,6	6 1'37.631
17	99	S. MARTIN	AUS	DFX Racing Ducati Pirelli	Ducati 998 RS	23	37'40.830	48.867	279,6	16 1'37.558
18	36	I. CLEMENTI	ITA	Kawasaki Bertocchi	Kawasaki ZX-7RR	23	38'15.961	1'23.998	268,4	5 1'38.542
19	46	M. SANCHINI	ITA	Kawasaki Bertocchi	Kawasaki ZX-7RR	23	38'17.806	1'25.843	267,8	5 1'39.051
20	69	T. MULOT	FRA	Pacific	Ducati 996 RS	23	38'28.476	1'36.513	271,8	22 1'39.423
21	5	M. HECKLES	GBR	Castrol Honda Rumi	Honda VTR 1000 SP2	22	37'16.270	1 Lap	267,1	16 1'39.851

---**Not Classified:**---

	No.	Rider	Nat	Team	Bike	Laps	Time	Gap	Speed	Fastest Lap
RET	70	Y. GYGER	SUI	White Endurance	Honda VTR 1000 SP1	12	20'28.713	11 Laps	262,5	11 1'40.432
RET	28	S. FOTI	ITA	Pedercini	Ducati 996 RS	12	23'39.369	11 Laps	276,0	5 1'38.679
RET	68	B. STEY	FRA	White Endurance	Honda VTR 1000 SP1	3	5'07.609	20 Laps	267,8	3 1'39.591

RACE 2

Laps 20 = 80,100 km - Avg. 149,923 km/h

	No.	Rider	Nat	Team	Bike	Laps	Time	Gap	Speed	Fastest Lap
1	1	T. BAYLISS	AUS	Ducati Infostrada	Ducati 998 F 02	20	32'03.384		282,5	16 1'35.541
2	41	N. HAGA	JPN	Playstation2-FGF Aprilia	Aprilia RSV 1000	20	32'04.562	1.178	281,8	3 1'35.372
3	2	C. EDWARDS	USA	Castrol Honda	Honda VTR 1000 SP2	20	32'05.669	2.285	283,3	7 1'35.800
4	155	B. BOSTROM	USA	Ducati L & M	Ducati 998 F 02	20	32'08.528	5.144	281,0	6 1'35.306
5	100	N. HODGSON	GBR	HM Plant Ducati	Ducati 998 F 01	20	32'20.766	17.382	281,8	4 1'35.934
6	14	H. IZUTSU	JPN	Kawasaki Racing	Kawasaki ZX-7RR	20	32'29.194	25.810	281,8	8 1'36.424
7	9	C. WALKER	GBR	Kawasaki Racing	Kawasaki ZX-7RR	20	32'35.121	31.737	274,6	8 1'36.735
8	33	J. BORJA	ESP	Spaziotel Racing	Ducati 998 RS	20	32'36.591	33.207	276,0	17 1'37.008
9	99	S. MARTIN	AUS	DFX Racing Ducati Pirelli	Ducati 998 RS	20	32'41.085	37.701	278,1	11 1'37.253
10	52	J. TOSELAND	GBR	HM Plant Ducati	Ducati 998 F 01	20	32'41.595	38.211	279,6	7 1'36.678
11	19	L. PEDERCINI	ITA	Pedercini	Ducati 998 RS	20	32'44.323	40.939	277,4	11 1'36.973
12	20	M. BORCIANI	ITA	Pedercini	Ducati 998 RS	20	32'45.224	41.840	278,1	4 1'37.370
13	36	I. CLEMENTI	ITA	Kawasaki Bertocchi	Kawasaki ZX-7RR	20	33'03.127	59.743	271,1	6 1'38.103
14	28	S. FOTI	ITA	Pedercini	Ducati 996 RS	20	33'03.415	1'00.031	274,6	6 1'38.356
15	46	M. SANCHINI	ITA	Kawasaki Bertocchi	Kawasaki ZX-7RR	20	33'09.494	1'06.110	270,5	7 1'38.617
16	69	T. MULOT	FRA	Pacific	Ducati 996 RS	20	33'28.008	1'24.624	269,1	15 1'39.326
17	68	B. STEY	FRA	White Endurance	Honda VTR 1000 SP1	20	33'37.544	1'34.160	267,1	6 1'39.374

---**Not Classified:**---

	No.	Rider	Nat	Team	Bike	Laps	Time	Gap	Speed	Fastest Lap
RET	5	M. HECKLES	GBR	Castrol Honda Rumi	Honda VTR 1000 SP2	18	30'10.821	2 Laps	267,8	14 1'39.521
RET	7	P. CHILI	ITA	Ducati NCR	Ducati 998 RS	9	14'46.277	11 Laps	275,3	6 1'36.363
RET	10	G. LAVILLA	ESP	Alstare Suzuki Corona	Suzuki GSX-R750 Y	8	13'02.515	12 Laps	280,3	7 1'36.192
RET	70	Y. GYGER	SUI	White Endurance	Honda VTR 1000 SP1	8	13'41.900	12 Laps	262,5	3 1'41.021
RET	11	R. XAUS	ESP	Ducati Infostrada	Ducati 998 F 02	7	11'18.795	13 Laps	278,9	7 1'35.556
RET	30	A. ANTONELLO	ITA	DFX Racing Ducati Pirelli	Ducati 998 RS	6	9'51.843	14 Laps	280,3	6 1'36.909

PHILLIP ISLAND - AUS
22-23-24 March, 2002

RACE 1

Laps 22 = 97,790 km - Avg. 170,061 km/h

	No.	Rider	Nat	Team	Bike	Laps	Time	Gap	Speed	Fastest Lap
1	1	T. BAYLISS	AUS	Ducati Infostrada	Ducati 998 F 02	22	34'30.102		300,8	12 1'33.451
2	2	C. EDWARDS	USA	Castrol Honda	Honda VTR 1000 SP2	22	34'32.571	2.469	300,8	13 1'33.382
3	11	R. XAUS	ESP	Ducati Infostrada	Ducati 998 F 02	22	34'40.162	10.060	299,2	9 1'33.597
4	155	B. BOSTROM	USA	Ducati L & M	Ducati 998 F 02	22	34'51.234	21.132	300,0	2 1'34.023
5	100	N. HODGSON	GBR	HM Plant Ducati	Ducati 998 F 01	22	34'51.320	21.218	304,2	3 1'33.899
6	14	H. IZUTSU	JPN	Kawasaki Racing	Kawasaki ZX-7RR	22	35'08.025	37.923	299,2	9 1'34.974
7	10	G. LAVILLA	ESP	Alstare Suzuki Corona	Suzuki GSX-R750 Y	22	35'08.111	38.009	300,0	18 1'35.069
8	52	J. TOSELAND	GBR	HM Plant Ducati	Ducati 998 F 01	22	35'11.240	41.138	298,3	14 1'35.123
9	9	C. WALKER	GBR	Kawasaki Racing	Kawasaki ZX-7RR	22	35'20.981	50.879	295,9	6 1'35.161
10	19	L. PEDERCINI	ITA	Pedercini	Ducati 998 RS	22	35'31.648	1'01.546	294,3	3 1'35.670
11	20	M. BORCIANI	ITA	Pedercini	Ducati 998 RS	22	35'36.470	1'06.368	294,3	12 1'36.119
12	33	J. BORJA	ESP	Spaziotel Racing	Ducati 998 RS	22	35'40.282	1'10.180	293,5	3 1'35.722
13	99	S. MARTIN	AUS	DFX Racing Ducati Pirelli	Ducati 998 RS	22	35'46.709	1'16.607	302,5	5 1'36.003
14	30	A. ANTONELLO	ITA	DFX Racing Ducati Pirelli	Ducati 998 RS	22	35'47.983	1'17.881	304,2	3 1'35.544
15	46	M. SANCHINI	ITA	Kawasaki Bertocchi	Kawasaki ZX-7RR	22	35'48.026	1'17.924	290,3	4 1'36.927
16	5	M. HECKLES	GBR	Castrol Honda Rumi	Honda VTR 1000 SP2	22	35'49.332	1'19.230	285,0	13 1'36.960

----------------------------------Not Classified:----------------------------------

	No.	Rider	Nat	Team	Bike	Laps	Time	Gap	Speed	Fastest Lap
RET	36	I. CLEMENTI	ITA	Kawasaki Bertocchi	Kawasaki ZX-7RR	21	34'07.248	1 Lap	285,0	4 1'35.809
RET	12	B. PARKES	AUS	Ducati NCR Parmalat	Ducati 998 RS	12	19'25.143	10 Laps	296,7	3 1'35.280
RET	7	P. CHILI	ITA	Ducati NCR Axo	Ducati 998 RS	12	20'12.593	10 Laps	300,8	3 1'35.363
RET	28	S. FOTI	ITA	Pedercini	Ducati 996 RS	10	16'16.317	12 Laps	295,1	7 1'36.609
RET	41	N. HAGA	JPN	Playstation2-FGF Aprilia	Aprilia RSV 1000	9	14'15.213	13 Laps	305,1	3 1'33.988
RET	68	B. STEY	FRA	White Endurance	Honda VTR 1000 SP1	4	6'41.640	18 Laps	289,5	3 1'37.976
RET	17	A. MAXWELL	AUS	Alistair Maxwell	Kawasaki ZX-7RR	0			108,5	

RACE 2

Laps 22 = 97,790 km - Avg. 169,608 km/h

	No.	Rider	Nat	Team	Bike	Laps	Time	Gap	Speed	Fastest Lap
1	1	T. BAYLISS	AUS	Ducati Infostrada	Ducati 998 F 02	22	34'35.633		297,5	18 1'33.773
2	2	C. EDWARDS	USA	Castrol Honda	Honda VTR 1000 SP2	22	34'38.105	2.472	300,8	4 1'33.700
3	11	R. XAUS	ESP	Ducati Infostrada	Ducati 998 F 02	22	34'45.315	9.682	299,2	4 1'33.735
4	100	N. HODGSON	GBR	HM Plant Ducati	Ducati 998 F 01	22	34'54.546	18.913	302,5	9 1'34.234
5	155	B. BOSTROM	USA	Ducati L & M	Ducati 998 F 02	22	34'54.577	18.944	308,6	4 1'34.000
6	41	N. HAGA	JPN	Playstation2-FGF Aprilia	Aprilia RSV 1000	22	34'55.206	19.573	309,5	4 1'34.239
7	52	J. TOSELAND	GBR	HM Plant Ducati	Ducati 998 F 01	22	35'08.589	32.956	295,9	9 1'35.297
8	10	G. LAVILLA	ESP	Alstare Suzuki Corona	Suzuki GSX-R750 Y	22	35'08.634	33.001	305,1	3 1'34.511
9	9	C. WALKER	GBR	Kawasaki Racing	Kawasaki ZX-7RR	22	35'08.718	33.085	295,9	2 1'34.993
10	33	J. BORJA	ESP	Spaziotel Racing	Ducati 998 RS	22	35'37.515	1'01.882	291,9	5 1'36.259
11	30	A. ANTONELLO	ITA	DFX Racing Ducati Pirelli	Ducati 998 RS	22	35'39.836	1'04.203	302,5	2 1'35.846
12	46	M. SANCHINI	ITA	Kawasaki Bertocchi	Kawasaki ZX-7RR	22	35'42.860	1'07.227	288,0	3 1'36.411
13	12	B. PARKES	AUS	Ducati NCR Parmalat	Ducati 998 RS	22	35'43.195	1'07.562	296,7	2 1'36.529
14	5	M. HECKLES	GBR	Castrol Honda Rumi	Honda VTR 1000 SP2	22	35'43.427	1'07.794	286,5	19 1'36.433
15	36	I. CLEMENTI	ITA	Kawasaki Bertocchi	Kawasaki ZX-7RR	22	35'45.036	1'09.403	285,7	4 1'36.621
16	68	B. STEY	FRA	White Endurance	Honda VTR 1000 SP1	21	34'40.919	1 Lap	285,7	3 1'37.388
17	17	A. MAXWELL	AUS	Alistair Maxwell	Kawasaki ZX-7RR	21	35'28.989	1 Lap	283,5	3 1'38.340

----------------------------------Not Classified:----------------------------------

	No.	Rider	Nat	Team	Bike	Laps	Time	Gap	Speed	Fastest Lap
RET	14	H. IZUTSU	JPN	Kawasaki Racing	Kawasaki ZX-7RR	16	25'22.632	6 Laps	300,8	4 1'34.076
RET	20	M. BORCIANI	ITA	Pedercini	Ducati 998 RS	15	24'26.524	7 Laps	293,5	10 1'36.680
RET	19	L. PEDERCINI	ITA	Pedercini	Ducati 998 RS	11	18'20.566	11 Laps	295,1	3 1'36.333
RET	7	P. CHILI	ITA	Ducati NCR Axo	Ducati 998 RS	8	12'50.173	14 Laps	300,8	2 1'34.667
RET	99	S. MARTIN	AUS	DFX Racing Ducati Pirelli	Ducati 998 RS	7	11'23.218	15 Laps	298,3	5 1'35.896
RET	28	S. FOTI	ITA	Pedercini	Ducati 996 RS	6	9'50.914	16 Laps	293,5	3 1'36.666

KYALAMI - SA

5-6-7 April 2002

RACE 1

Laps 25 = 106,575 km - Avg. 148,607 km/h

	No.	Rider	Nat	Team	Bike	Laps	Time	Gap	Speed	Fastest Lap
1	1	T. **BAYLISS**	AUS	Ducati Infostrada	Ducati 998 F 02	25	43'01.781		238,9	2 1'42.326
2	2	C. **EDWARDS**	USA	Castrol Honda	Honda VTR 1000 SP2	25	43'05.900	**4.119**	237,4	10 1'42.551
3	11	R. **XAUS**	ESP	Ducati Infostrada	Ducati 998 F 02	25	43'08.317	**6.536**	237,9	3 1'42.690
4	155	B. **BOSTROM**	USA	Ducati L & M	Ducati 998 F 02	25	43'13.764	**11.983**	233,3	2 1'42.652
5	100	N. **HODGSON**	GBR	HM Plant Ducati	Ducati 998 F 01	25	43'18.605	**16.824**	240,5	2 1'42.574
6	52	J. **TOSELAND**	GBR	HM Plant Ducati	Ducati 998 F 01	25	43'31.325	**29.544**	235,8	11 1'43.626
7	14	H. **IZUTSU**	JPN	Kawasaki Racing	Kawasaki ZX-7RR	25	43'39.161	**37.380**	235,8	13 1'43.669
8	9	C. **WALKER**	GBR	Kawasaki Racing	Kawasaki ZX-7RR	25	43'49.079	**47.298**	231,8	2 1'43.653
9	33	J. **BORJA**	ESP	Spaziotel Racing	Ducati 998 RS	25	43'56.353	**54.572**	235,8	17 1'44.695
10	20	M. **BORCIANI**	ITA	Pedercini	Ducati 998 RS	25	43'56.822	**55.041**	233,8	17 1'44.840
11	12	B. **PARKES**	AUS	Ducati NCR Parmalat	Ducati 998 RS	25	44'20.069	**1'18.288**	234,3	3 1'45.077
12	28	S. **FOTI**	ITA	Pedercini	Ducati 996 RS	25	44'31.713	**1'29.932**	231,8	2 1'45.210
13	46	M. **SANCHINI**	ITA	Kawasaki Bertocchi	Kawasaki ZX-7RR	24	43'06.408	**1 Lap**	225,9	4 1'46.450
14	68	B. **STEY**	FRA	White Endurance	Honda VTR 1000 SP1	24	43'10.744	**1 Lap**	226,9	4 1'46.531

---Not Classified:---

	No.	Rider	Nat	Team	Bike	Laps	Time	Gap	Speed	Fastest Lap
RET	41	N. **HAGA**	JPN	Playstation2-FGF Aprilia	Aprilia RSV 1000	17	29'34.086	**8 Laps**	241,6	2 1'42.197
RET	19	L. **PEDERCINI**	ITA	Pedercini	Ducati 998 RS	12	21'00.181	**13 Laps**	231,3	4 1'44.145
RET	10	G. **LAVILLA**	ESP	Alstare Suzuki Corona	Suzuki GSX-R750 Y	12	21'00.476	**13 Laps**	233,3	8 1'43.827
RET	23	J. **MRKYVKA**	CZE	JM Racing	Ducati 996 RS	8	14'42.090	**17 Laps**	224,1	2 1'48.105
RET	99	S. **MARTIN**	AUS	DFX Racing Ducati Pirelli	Ducati 998 RS	6	10'37.513	**19 Laps**	233,8	5 1'44.978
RET	30	A. **ANTONELLO**	ITA	DFX Racing Ducati Pirelli	Ducati 998 RS	1	1'52.920	**24 Laps**	226,4	
NS	5	M. **HECKLES**	GBR	Castrol Honda Rumi	Honda VTR 1000 SP2					
NS	7	P. **CHILI**	ITA	Ducati NCR Axo	Ducati 998 RS					

RACE 2

Laps 25 = 106,575 km - Avg. 148,882 km/h

	No.	Rider	Nat	Team	Bike	Laps	Time	Gap	Speed	Fastest Lap
1	1	T. **BAYLISS**	AUS	Ducati Infostrada	Ducati 998 F 02	25	42'57.014		239,5	4 1'42.415
2	11	R. **XAUS**	ESP	Ducati Infostrada	Ducati 998 F 02	25	42'59.687	**2.673**	238,9	5 1'42.369
3	2	C. **EDWARDS**	USA	Castrol Honda	Honda VTR 1000 SP2	25	43'03.404	**6.390**	236,8	5 1'42.618
4	100	N. **HODGSON**	GBR	HM Plant Ducati	Ducati 998 F 01	25	43'03.788	**6.774**	239,5	3 1'42.749
5	155	B. **BOSTROM**	USA	Ducati L & M	Ducati 998 F 02	25	43'06.368	**9.354**	234,8	3 1'42.444
6	41	N. **HAGA**	JPN	Playstation2-FGF Aprilia	Aprilia RSV 1000	25	43'08.997	**11.983**	244,3	3 1'42.178
7	14	H. **IZUTSU**	JPN	Kawasaki Racing	Kawasaki ZX-7RR	25	43'24.674	**27.660**	238,9	7 1'43.087
8	52	J. **TOSELAND**	GBR	HM Plant Ducati	Ducati 998 F 01	25	43'25.890	**28.876**	235,8	16 1'43.595
9	9	C. **WALKER**	GBR	Kawasaki Racing	Kawasaki ZX-7RR	25	43'37.795	**40.781**	230,3	5 1'43.758
10	33	J. **BORJA**	ESP	Spaziotel Racing	Ducati 998 RS	25	43'40.269	**43.255**	235,8	3 1'43.829
11	10	G. **LAVILLA**	ESP	Alstare Suzuki Corona	Suzuki GSX-R750 Y	25	43'43.392	**46.378**	232,3	5 1'43.631
12	19	L. **PEDERCINI**	ITA	Pedercini	Ducati 998 RS	25	43'53.429	**56.415**	232,8	5 1'43.942
13	20	M. **BORCIANI**	ITA	Pedercini	Ducati 998 RS	25	43'58.815	**1'01.801**	233,8	3 1'44.655
14	12	B. **PARKES**	AUS	Ducati NCR Parmalat	Ducati 998 RS	25	44'15.014	**1'18.000**	233,3	5 1'44.942
15	28	S. **FOTI**	ITA	Pedercini	Ducati 996 RS	25	44'30.178	**1'33.164**	231,8	4 1'45.761
16	46	M. **SANCHINI**	ITA	Kawasaki Bertocchi	Kawasaki ZX-7RR	24	43'20.047	**1 Lap**	225,5	7 1'46.008
17	68	B. **STEY**	FRA	White Endurance	Honda VTR 1000 SP1	24	43'21.563	**1 Lap**	227,4	3 1'47.203
18	23	J. **MRKYVKA**	CZE	JM Racing	Ducati 996 RS	24	43'22.313	**1 Lap**	225,9	4 1'47.445

---Not Classified:---

	No.	Rider	Nat	Team	Bike	Laps	Time	Gap	Speed	Fastest Lap
RET	30	A. **ANTONELLO**	ITA	DFX Racing Ducati Pirelli	Ducati 998 RS	14	24'50.611	**11 Laps**	235,8	7 1'45.164
RET	99	S. **MARTIN**	AUS	DFX Racing Ducati Pirelli	Ducati 998 RS	4	7'08.521	**21 Laps**	233,8	4 1'44.915
NS	7	P. **CHILI**	ITA	Ducati NCR Axo	Ducati 998 RS					
NS	5	M. **HECKLES**	GBR	Castrol Honda Rumi	Honda VTR 1000 SP2					

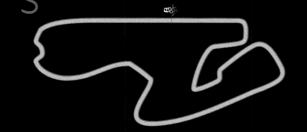

SUGO – JPN

19-20-21 April, 2002

RACE 1

Laps 25 = 93,425 km - Avg. 149,845 km/h

	No.	Rider	Nat	Team	Bike	Laps	Time	Gap	Speed	Fastest Lap
1	2	C. EDWARDS	USA	Castrol Honda	Honda VTR 1000 SP2	25	37'24.515		271,4	9 1'29.281
2	42	M. TAMADA	JPN	Cabin Honda	Honda VTR 1000 SP2	25	37'24.676	0.161	275,5	11 1'29.288
3	41	N. HAGA	JPN	Playstation2-FGF Aprilia	Aprilia RSV 1000	25	37'29.001	4.486	276,2	4 1'29.175
4	100	N. HODGSON	GBR	HM Plant Ducati	Ducati 998 F 01	25	37'36.770	12.255	272,7	10 1'29.397
5	1	T. BAYLISS	AUS	Ducati Infostrada	Ducati 998 F 02	25	37'45.828	21.313	273,4	3 1'29.726
6	49	A. YANAGAWA	JPN	Kawasaki Racing	Kawasaki ZX-7RR	25	37'47.392	22.877	272,7	3 1'29.704
7	155	B. BOSTROM	USA	Ducati L & M	Ducati 998 F 02	25	37'47.776	23.261	270,7	7 1'29.725
8	43	W. YOSHIKAWA	JPN	YSP Racing & PRESTO	Yamaha YZF R7	25	37'50.874	26.359	270,0	6 1'30.049
9	52	J. TOSELAND	GBR	HM Plant Ducati	Ducati 998 F 01	25	37'53.597	29.082	266,0	22 1'30.314
10	45	T. TSUJIMURA	JPN	YSP Racing & PRESTO	Yamaha YZF R7	25	37'54.863	30.348	266,7	12 1'30.326
11	9	C. WALKER	GBR	Kawasaki Racing	Kawasaki ZX-7RR	25	37'55.537	31.022	264,7	9 1'30.201
12	10	G. LAVILLA	ESP	Alstare Suzuki Corona	Suzuki GSX-R750 Y	25	38'06.876	42.361	274,8	6 1'30.466
13	32	E. BOSTROM	USA	Kawasaki Racing	Kawasaki ZX-7RR	25	38'07.883	43.368	265,4	4 1'30.538
14	33	J. BORJA	ESP	Spaziotel Racing	Ducati 998 RS	25	38'08.649	44.134	268,7	3 1'30.764
15	48	Y. TAKEDA	JPN	Sakurai Honda	Honda VTR 1000 SP2	25	38'08.787	44.272	268,0	3 1'30.732
16	19	L. PEDERCINI	ITA	Pedercini	Ducati 998 RS	25	38'41.742	1'17.227	263,4	5 1'31.656
17	99	S. MARTIN	AUS	DFX Racing Ducati Pirelli	Ducati 998 RS	25	38'44.488	1'19.973	267,3	6 1'31.935
18	36	I. CLEMENTI	ITA	Kawasaki Bertocchi	Kawasaki ZX-7RR	25	38'49.028	1'24.513	256,5	9 1'32.237
19	47	K. NAKAMURA	JPN	Blue Helmet MSC	Honda VTR 1000 SP2	25	38'57.712	1'33.197	266,0	3 1'32.339
20	46	M. SANCHINI	ITA	Kawasaki Bertocchi	Kawasaki ZX-7RR	24	37'24.677	1 Lap	259,0	10 1'32.738
21	5	M. HECKLES	GBR	Castrol Honda Rumi	Honda VTR 1000 SP2	24	37'51.570	1 Lap	260,2	11 1'32.138

---Not Classified:---

	No.	Rider	Nat	Team	Bike	Laps	Time	Gap	Speed	Fastest Lap
RET	11	R. XAUS	ESP	Ducati Infostrada	Ducati 998 F 02	17	25'38.256	8 Laps	270,7	6 1'29.521
RET	12	B. PARKES	AUS	Ducati NCR Parmalat	Ducati 998 RS	8	13'09.088	17 Laps	249,4	7 1'32.558
RET	30	A. ANTONELLO	ITA	DFX Racing Ducati Pirelli	Ducati 998 RS	4	6'39.860	21 Laps	268,0	3 1'33.629
RET	20	M. BORCIANI	ITA	Pedercini	Ducati 998 RS	1	1'39.942	24 Laps	257,1	
NS	14	H. IZUTSU	JPN	Kawasaki Racing	Kawasaki ZX-7RR					

RACE 2

Laps 25 = 93,425 km - Avg. 149,704 km/h

	No.	Rider	Nat	Team	Bike	Laps	Time	Gap	Speed	Fastest Lap
1	42	M. TAMADA	JPN	Cabin Honda	Honda VTR 1000 SP2	25	37'26.628		275,5	17 1'29.108
2	2	C. EDWARDS	USA	Castrol Honda	Honda VTR 1000 SP2	25	37'29.925	3.297	272,7	6 1'29.406
3	100	N. HODGSON	GBR	HM Plant Ducati	Ducati 998 F 01	25	37'30.097	3.469	272,0	6 1'29.362
4	1	T. BAYLISS	AUS	Ducati Infostrada	Ducati 998 F 02	25	37'30.308	3.680	273,4	5 1'29.369
5	41	N. HAGA	JPN	Playstation2-FGF Aprilia	Aprilia RSV 1000	25	37'34.084	7.456	276,9	4 1'29.128
6	49	A. YANAGAWA	JPN	Kawasaki Racing	Kawasaki ZX-7RR	25	37'36.190	9.562	272,0	11 1'29.766
7	155	B. BOSTROM	USA	Ducati L & M	Ducati 998 F 02	25	37'39.361	12.733	270,7	6 1'29.444
8	43	W. YOSHIKAWA	JPN	YSP Racing & PRESTO	Yamaha YZF R7	25	37'47.325	20.697	272,0	3 1'29.894
9	11	R. XAUS	ESP	Ducati Infostrada	Ducati 998 F 02	25	37'54.849	28.221	269,3	10 1'29.900
10	45	T. TSUJIMURA	JPN	YSP Racing & PRESTO	Yamaha YZF R7	25	37'55.163	28.535	266,0	12 1'29.907
11	52	J. TOSELAND	GBR	HM Plant Ducati	Ducati 998 F 01	25	38'00.052	33.424	266,7	11 1'30.206
12	10	G. LAVILLA	ESP	Alstare Suzuki Corona	Suzuki GSX-R750 Y	25	38'00.550	33.922	274,8	9 1'30.188
13	9	C. WALKER	GBR	Kawasaki Racing	Kawasaki ZX-7RR	25	38'01.249	34.621	264,1	2 1'30.498
14	32	E. BOSTROM	USA	Kawasaki Racing	Kawasaki ZX-7RR	25	38'05.189	38.561	266,7	13 1'30.595
15	33	J. BORJA	ESP	Spaziotel Racing	Ducati 998 RS	25	38'13.500	46.872	269,3	4 1'30.947
16	48	Y. TAKEDA	JPN	Sakurai Honda	Honda VTR 1000 SP2	25	38'15.735	49.107	269,3	7 1'30.669
17	20	M. BORCIANI	ITA	Pedercini	Ducati 998 RS	25	38'36.813	1'10.185	268,0	6 1'31.716
18	19	L. PEDERCINI	ITA	Pedercini	Ducati 998 RS	25	38'38.131	1'11.503	262,8	16 1'31.670
19	36	I. CLEMENTI	ITA	Kawasaki Bertocchi	Kawasaki ZX-7RR	25	38'41.360	1'14.732	259,6	10 1'31.980
20	99	S. MARTIN	AUS	DFX Racing Ducati Pirelli	Ducati 998 RS	25	38'42.822	1'16.194	268,0	10 1'31.890
21	47	K. NAKAMURA	JPN	Blue Helmet MSC	Honda VTR 1000 SP2	25	38'58.150	1'31.522	268,0	10 1'32.274
22	46	M. SANCHINI	ITA	Kawasaki Bertocchi	Kawasaki ZX-7RR	24	37'32.159	1 Lap	259,0	9 1'32.570

---Not Classified:---

	No.	Rider	Nat	Team	Bike	Laps	Time	Gap	Speed	Fastest Lap
RET	5	M. HECKLES	GBR	Castrol Honda Rumi	Honda VTR 1000 SP2	17	26'28.885	8 Laps	257,8	5 1'32.173
RET	12	B. PARKES	AUS	Ducati NCR Parmalat	Ducati 998 RS	5	8'05.211	20 Laps	252,3	4 1'33.406
NS	30	A. ANTONELLO	ITA	DFX Racing Ducati Pirelli	Ducati 998 RS					
NS	14	H. IZUTSU	JPN	Kawasaki Racing	Kawasaki ZX-7RR					

MONZA - ITA

10-11-12 May, 2002

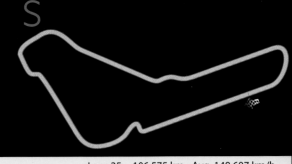

RACE 1

Laps 25 = 106,575 km - Avg. 148,607 km/h

	No.	Rider	Nat	Team	Bike	Laps	Time	Gap	Speed	Fastest Lap
1	1	T. **BAYLISS**	AUS	Ducati Infostrada	Ducati 998 F 02	25	43'01.781		238,9	2 1'42.326
2	2	C. **EDWARDS**	USA	Castrol Honda	Honda VTR 1000 SP2	25	43'05.900	**4.119**	237,4	10 1'42.551
3	11	R. **XAUS**	ESP	Ducati Infostrada	Ducati 998 F 02	25	43'08.317	**6.536**	237,9	3 1'42.690
4	155	B. **BOSTROM**	USA	Ducati L & M	Ducati 998 F 02	25	43'13.764	**11.983**	233,3	2 1'42.652
5	100	N. **HODGSON**	GBR	HM Plant Ducati	Ducati 998 F 01	25	43'18.605	**16.824**	240,5	2 1'42.574
6	52	J. **TOSELAND**	GBR	HM Plant Ducati	Ducati 998 F 01	25	43'31.325	**29.544**	235,8	11 1'43.626
7	14	H. **IZUTSU**	JPN	Kawasaki Racing	Kawasaki ZX-7RR	25	43'39.161	**37.380**	235,8	13 1'43.669
8	9	C. **WALKER**	GBR	Kawasaki Racing	Kawasaki ZX-7RR	25	43'49.079	**47.298**	231,8	2 1'43.653
9	33	J. **BORJA**	ESP	Spaziotel Racing	Ducati 998 RS	25	43'56.353	**54.572**	235,8	17 1'44.695
10	20	M. **BORCIANI**	ITA	Pedercini	Ducati 998 RS	25	43'56.822	**55.041**	233,8	17 1'44.840
11	12	B. **PARKES**	AUS	Ducati NCR Parmalat	Ducati 998 RS	25	44'20.069	**1'18.288**	234,3	3 1'45.077
12	28	S. **FOTI**	ITA	Pedercini	Ducati 996 RS	25	44'31.713	**1'29.932**	231,8	2 1'45.210
13	46	M. **SANCHINI**	ITA	Kawasaki Bertocchi	Kawasaki ZX-7RR	24	43'06.408	**1 Lap**	225,9	4 1'46.450
14	68	B. **STEY**	FRA	White Endurance	Honda VTR 1000 SP1	24	43'10.744	**1 Lap**	226,9	4 1'46.531

---Not Classified:---

	No.	Rider	Nat	Team	Bike	Laps	Time	Gap	Speed	Fastest Lap
RET	41	N. **HAGA**	JPN	Playstation2-FGF Aprilia	Aprilia RSV 1000	17	29'34.086	**8 Laps**	241,6	2 1'42.197
RET	19	L. **PEDERCINI**	ITA	Pedercini	Ducati 998 RS	12	21'00.181	**13 Laps**	231,3	4 1'44.145
RET	10	G. **LAVILLA**	ESP	Alstare Suzuki Corona	Suzuki GSX-R750 Y	12	21'00.476	**13 Laps**	233,3	8 1'43.827
RET	23	J. **MRKYVKA**	CZE	JM Racing	Ducati 996 RS	8	14'42.090	**17 Laps**	224,1	2 1'48.105
RET	99	S. **MARTIN**	AUS	DFX Racing Ducati Pirelli	Ducati 998 RS	6	10'37.513	**19 Laps**	233,8	5 1'44.978
RET	30	A. **ANTONELLO**	ITA	DFX Racing Ducati Pirelli	Ducati 998 RS	1	1'52.920	**24 Laps**	226,4	
NS	5	M. **HECKLES**	GBR	Castrol Honda Rumi	Honda VTR 1000 SP2					
NS	7	P. **CHILI**	ITA	Ducati NCR Axo	Ducati 998 RS					

RACE 2

Laps 18 = 104,274 km - Avg. 190,388 km/h

	No.	Rider	Nat	Team	Bike	Laps	Time	Gap	Speed	Fastest Lap
1	1	T. **BAYLISS**	AUS	Ducati Infostrada	Ducati 998 F 02	18	32'51.693		297,7	13 1'48.570
2	2	C. **EDWARDS**	USA	Castrol Honda	Honda VTR 1000 SP2	18	32'53.919	**2.226**	293,0	5 1'49.032
3	41	N. **HAGA**	JPN	Playstation2-FGF Aprilia	Aprilia RSV 1000	18	32'53.960	**2.267**	283,2	11 1'49.000
4	100	N. **HODGSON**	GBR	HM Plant Ducati	Ducati 998 F 01	18	32'53.984	**2.291**	302,6	6 1'49.039
5	10	G. **LAVILLA**	ESP	Alstare Suzuki Corona	Suzuki GSX-R750 Y	18	33'13.537	**21.844**	294,5	4 1'49.703
6	19	L. **PEDERCINI**	ITA	Pedercini	Ducati 998 RS	18	33'13.651	**21.958**	289,1	4 1'49.439
7	32	E. **BOSTROM**	USA	Kawasaki Racing	Kawasaki ZX-7RR	18	33'14.026	**22.333**	286,9	4 1'49.919
8	12	B. **PARKES**	AUS	Ducati NCR Parmalat	Ducati 998 RS	18	33'26.178	**34.485**	278,2	11 1'50.361
9	155	B. **BOSTROM**	USA	Ducati L & M	Ducati 998 F 02	18	33'26.235	**34.542**	294,5	17 1'48.902
10	9	C. **WALKER**	GBR	Kawasaki Racing	Kawasaki ZX-7RR	18	33'26.315	**34.622**	294,5	3 1'50.202
11	99	S. **MARTIN**	AUS	DFX Racing Ducati Pirelli	Ducati 998 RS	18	33'34.441	**42.748**	292,2	9 1'51.099
12	28	S. **FOTI**	ITA	Pedercini	Ducati 996 RS	18	33'52.791	**1'01.098**	287,6	5 1'51.644
13	46	M. **SANCHINI**	ITA	Kawasaki Bertocchi	Kawasaki ZX-7RR	18	33'59.235	**1'07.542**	284,7	8 1'51.805
14	36	I. **CLEMENTI**	ITA	Kawasaki Bertocchi	Kawasaki ZX-7RR	18	34'10.312	**1'18.619**	276,8	8 1'52.033
15	50	A. **VALIA**	ITA	Ass. Sportiva Bassani	Ducati 996 R	18	34'13.618	**1'21.925**	289,1	4 1'52.958
16	113	P. **BLORA**	ITA	Pacific	Ducati 996 RS	18	34'15.381	**1'23.688**	288,4	2 1'53.035
17	6	P. **GODDARD**	AUS	Benelli Sport	Benelli Tornado 900	18	34'28.798	**1'37.105**	280,3	17 1'54.148
18	5	M. **HECKLES**	GBR	Castrol Honda Rumi	Honda VTR 1000 SP2	17	34'07.447	**1 Lap**	266,7	7 1'55.604

---Not Classified:---

	No.	Rider	Nat	Team	Bike	Laps	Time	Gap	Speed	Fastest Lap
RET	33	J. **BORJA**	ESP	Spaziotel Racing	Ducati 998 RS	15	27'54.373	**3 Laps**	295,3	3 1'50.628
RET	20	M. **BORCIANI**	ITA	Pedercini	Ducati 998 RS	12	23'05.111	**6 Laps**	286,1	2 1'50.837
RET	30	A. **ANTONELLO**	ITA	DFX Racing Ducati Pirelli	Ducati 998 RS	9	17'10.477	**9 Laps**	295,3	5 1'51.207
RET	7	P. **CHILI**	ITA	Ducati NCR Axo	Ducati 998 RS	6	11'28.247	**12 Laps**	292,2	2 1'49.103
RET	93	C. **CALIUMI**	ITA	Pedercini	Ducati 996 RS	6	11'32.114	**12 Laps**	276,8	3 1'53.529
RET	52	J. **TOSELAND**	GBR	HM Plant Ducati	Ducati 998 F 01	5	9'10.770	**13 Laps**	284,7	5 1'49.344
RET	69	T. **MULOT**	FRA	Pacific	Ducati 996 RS	5	9'56.979	**13 Laps**	262,3	2 1'55.275
RET	68	B. **STEY**	FRA	White Endurance	Honda VTR 1000 SP1	4	8'46.888	**14 Laps**	278,2	2 1'53.506
RET	11	R. **XAUS**	ESP	Ducati Infostrada	Ducati 998 F 02	2	3'41.447	**16 Laps**	262,9	2 1'49.188

SILVERSTONE - GBR
24-25-26 May, 2002

RACE 1

Laps 20 = 101,880 km - Avg. 140,658 km/h

	No.	Rider	Nat	Team	Bike	Laps	Time	Gap	Speed	Fastest Lap
1	2	C. EDWARDS	USA	Castrol Honda	Honda VTR 1000 SP2	20	43'27.508		266,9	2 2'05.554
2	41	N. HAGA	JPN	Playstation2-FGF Aprilia	Aprilia RSV 1000	20	43'34.866	7.358	267,1	3 2'08.257
3	100	N. HODGSON	GBR	HM Plant Ducati	Ducati 998 F 01	20	44'00.498	32.990	265,7	2 2'07.322
4	7	P. CHILI	ITA	Ducati NCR Axo	Ducati 998 RS	20	44'19.106	51.598	266,4	3 2'07.227
5	1	T. BAYLISS	AUS	Ducati Infostrada	Ducati 998 F 02	20	44'22.230	54.722	264,3	2 2'05.551
6	5	M. HECKLES	GBR	Castrol Honda Rumi	Honda VTR 1000 SP2	20	44'28.636	1'01.128	253,7	6 2'09.936
7	155	B. BOSTROM	USA	Ducati L & M	Ducati 998 F 02	20	44'30.139	1'02.631	265,5	2 2'09.333
8	11	R. XAUS	ESP	Ducati Infostrada	Ducati 998 F 02	20	44'40.033	1'12.525	261,6	2 2'10.627
9	55	S. BYRNE	GBR	Renegade Ducati	Ducati 998 RS	20	44'42.734	1'15.226	261,4	2 2'09.127
10	52	J. TOSELAND	GBR	HM Plant Ducati	Ducati 998 F 01	20	44'51.178	1'23.670	264,3	2 2'08.930
11	32	E. BOSTROM	USA	Kawasaki Racing	Kawasaki ZX-7RR	20	44'56.126	1'28.618	261,1	20 2'12.923
12	54	M. RUTTER	GBR	Renegade Ducati	Ducati 998 RS	20	44'56.352	1'28.844	265,0	2 2'10.241
13	6	P. GODDARD	AUS	Benelli Sport	Benelli Tornado 900	20	45'02.106	1'34.598	251,2	2 2'11.965
14	9	C. WALKER	GBR	Kawasaki Racing	Kawasaki ZX-7RR	20	45'27.802	2'00.294	259,6	2 2'08.665
15	46	M. SANCHINI	ITA	Kawasaki Bertocchi	Kawasaki ZX-7RR	19	43'38.250	1 Lap	247,9	14 2'14.613
16	56	D. ELLISON	GBR	D & B Racing	Ducati 996 RS	19	44'47.562	1 Lap	255,6	3 2'15.496

---Not Classified:---

	No.	Rider	Nat	Team	Bike	Laps	Time	Gap	Speed	Fastest Lap
RET	36	I. CLEMENTI	ITA	Kawasaki Bertocchi	Kawasaki ZX-7RR	18	42'04.429	2 Laps	252,0	2 2'13.004
RET	53	S. HISLOP	GBR	Monster Mob Ducati	Ducati 998 RS	10	22'41.120	10 Laps	261,6	2 2'10.023
RET	57	G. RICHARDS	GBR	Hawk Kawasaki	Kawasaki ZX-7RR	9	20'04.875	11 Laps	258,9	2 2'11.141
RET	12	B. PARKES	AUS	Ducati NCR Parmalat	Ducati 998 RS	9	20'53.590	11 Laps	257,4	2 2'13.637
RET	10	G. LAVILLA	ESP	Alstare Suzuki Corona	Suzuki GSX-R750 Y	8	18'29.797	12 Laps	237,0	5 2'16.235
RET	28	S. FOTI	ITA	Pedercini	Ducati 996 RS	8	20'03.454	12 Laps	248,1	2 2'22.662
RET	33	J. BORJA	ESP	Spaziotel Racing	Ducati 998 RS	7	15'25.223	13 Laps	256,3	4 2'10.022
RET	23	J. MRKYVKA	CZE	JM Racing	Ducati 996 RS	4	9'03.163	16 Laps	261,6	2 2'13.394
RET	99	S. MARTIN	AUS	DFX Racing Ducati Pirelli	Ducati 998 RS	3	6'39.225	17 Laps	260,9	3 2'11.547
RET	19	L. PEDERCINI	ITA	Pedercini	Ducati 998 RS	3	7'25.329	17 Laps	237,0	2 2'25.559
RET	30	A. ANTONELLO	ITA	DFX Racing Ducati Pirelli	Ducati 998 RS	3	8'45.170	17 Laps	255,8	3 2'25.555
RET	20	M. BORCIANI	ITA	Pedercini	Ducati 998 RS	1	3'37.569	19 Laps	222,4	

RACE 2

Laps 20 = 101,880 km - Avg. 147,862 km/h

	No.	Rider	Nat	Team	Bike	Laps	Time	Gap	Speed	Fastest Lap
1	1	T. BAYLISS	AUS	Ducati Infostrada	Ducati 998 F 02	20	41'20.474		267,6	18 2'02.145
2	2	C. EDWARDS	USA	Castrol Honda	Honda VTR 1000 SP2	20	41'25.383	4.909	272,2	16 2'02.220
3	11	R. XAUS	ESP	Ducati Infostrada	Ducati 998 F 02	20	41'37.130	16.656	265,3	16 2'03.064
4	9	C. WALKER	GBR	Kawasaki Racing	Kawasaki ZX-7RR	20	42'18.909	58.435	259,3	11 2'05.459
5	55	S. BYRNE	GBR	Renegade Ducati	Ducati 998 RS	20	42'21.540	1'01.066	266,4	5 2'05.866
6	100	N. HODGSON	GBR	HM Plant Ducati	Ducati 998 F 01	20	42'32.455	1'11.981	266,4	16 2'06.360
7	33	J. BORJA	ESP	Spaziotel Racing	Ducati 998 RS	20	42'35.886	1'15.412	259,3	8 2'05.995
8	155	B. BOSTROM	USA	Ducati L & M	Ducati 998 F 02	20	42'37.796	1'17.322	264,1	19 2'05.769
9	52	J. TOSELAND	GBR	HM Plant Ducati	Ducati 998 F 01	20	42'45.360	1'24.886	262,5	17 2'07.089
10	41	N. HAGA	JPN	Playstation2-FGF Aprilia	Aprilia RSV 1000	20	43'01.781	1'41.307	267,8	5 2'07.265
11	7	P. CHILI	ITA	Ducati NCR Axo	Ducati 998 RS	20	43'15.792	1'55.318	267,8	17 2'04.942
12	12	B. PARKES	AUS	Ducati NCR Parmalat	Ducati 998 RS	20	43'18.242	1'57.768	264,3	20 2'05.496
13	30	A. ANTONELLO	ITA	DFX Racing Ducati Pirelli	Ducati 998 RS	20	43'20.834	2'00.360	265,7	19 2'07.499
14	10	G. LAVILLA	ESP	Alstare Suzuki Corona	Suzuki GSX-R750 Y	19	41'27.499	1 Lap	257,1	18 2'08.767
15	6	P. GODDARD	AUS	Benelli Sport	Benelli Tornado 900	19	41'29.601	1 Lap	251,0	9 2'09.323
16	32	E. BOSTROM	USA	Kawasaki Racing	Kawasaki ZX-7RR	19	41'34.591	1 Lap	261,4	17 2'09.233
17	23	J. MRKYVKA	CZE	JM Racing	Ducati 996 RS	19	41'35.236	1 Lap	259,3	19 2'08.313
18	36	I. CLEMENTI	ITA	Kawasaki Bertocchi	Kawasaki ZX-7RR	19	42'09.828	1 Lap	253,5	11 2'11.093
19	99	S. MARTIN	AUS	DFX Racing Ducati Pirelli	Ducati 998 RS	19	42'35.550	1 Lap	257,8	16 2'12.261

---Not Classified:---

	No.	Rider	Nat	Team	Bike	Laps	Time	Gap	Speed	Fastest Lap
RET	19	L. PEDERCINI	ITA	Pedercini	Ducati 998 RS	17	37'02.453	3 Laps	258,7	15 2'09.281
RET	57	G. RICHARDS	GBR	Hawk Kawasaki	Kawasaki ZX-7RR	13	28'46.030	7 Laps	257,4	12 2'10.280
RET	28	S. FOTI	ITA	Pedercini	Ducati 996 RS	13	29'24.287	7 Laps	255,2	9 2'12.592
RET	46	M. SANCHINI	ITA	Kawasaki Bertocchi	Kawasaki ZX-7RR	9	19'44.559	11 Laps	250,7	9 2'09.625
RET	54	M. RUTTER	GBR	Renegade Ducati	Ducati 998 RS	7	14'51.555	13 Laps	265,5	7 2'04.695
RET	5	M. HECKLES	GBR	Castrol Honda Rumi	Honda VTR 1000 SP2	5	10'59.187	15 Laps	253,3	5 2'08.221
RET	20	M. BORCIANI	ITA	Pedercini	Ducati 998 RS	4	9'36.505	16 Laps	255,6	3 2'20.261
RET	56	D. ELLISON	GBR	D & B Racing	Ducati 996 RS	1	2'20.697	19 Laps	252,8	
RET	53	S. HISLOP	GBR	Monster Mob Ducati	Ducati 998 RS	1	2'30.064	19 Laps	228,4	

LAUSITZ - GER
7-8-9 June, 2002

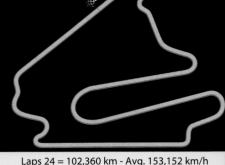

RACE 1

Laps 24 = 102,360 km - Avg. 153,152 km/h

	No.	Rider	Nat	Team	Bike	Laps	Time	Gap	Speed	Fastest Lap
1	1	T. **BAYLISS**	AUS	Ducati Infostrada	Ducati 998 F 02	24	40'06.073		270,2	5 1'39.704
2	2	C. **EDWARDS**	USA	Castrol Honda	Honda VTR 1000 SP2	24	40'06.724	**0.651**	270,9	6 1'39.797
3	11	R. **XAUS**	ESP	Ducati Infostrada	Ducati 998 F 02	24	40'25.039	**18.966**	267,5	10 1'40.399
4	41	N. **HAGA**	JPN	Playstation2-FGF Aprilia	Aprilia RSV 1000	24	40'29.555	**23.482**	277,9	11 1'40.320
5	155	B. **BOSTROM**	USA	Ducati L & M	Ducati 998 F 02	24	40'33.893	**27.820**	283,8	10 1'40.563
6	7	P. **CHILI**	ITA	Ducati NCR Axo	Ducati 998 RS	24	40'41.715	**35.642**	266,2	11 1'40.778
7	52	J. **TOSELAND**	GBR	HM Plant Ducati	Ducati 998 F 01	24	40'46.587	**40.514**	266,9	5 1'41.321
8	10	G. **LAVILLA**	ESP	Alstare Suzuki Corona	Suzuki GSX-R750 Y	24	40'53.169	**47.096**	273,7	5 1'41.284
9	99	S. **MARTIN**	AUS	DFX Racing Ducati Pirelli	Ducati 998 RS	24	40'53.600	**47.527**	270,2	8 1'41.430
10	19	L. **PEDERCINI**	ITA	Pedercini	Ducati 998 RS	24	41'15.525	**1'09.452**	262,3	6 1'42.443
11	12	B. **PARKES**	AUS	Ducati NCR Parmalat	Ducati 998 RS	24	41'15.696	**1'09.623**	257,9	12 1'42.218
12	20	M. **BORCIANI**	ITA	Pedercini	Ducati 998 RS	24	41'18.979	**1'12.906**	267,5	9 1'42.387
13	30	A. **ANTONELLO**	ITA	DFX Racing Ducati Pirelli	Ducati 998 RS	24	41'31.170	**1'25.097**	269,5	12 1'42.427
14	46	M. **SANCHINI**	ITA	Kawasaki Bertocchi	Kawasaki ZX-7RR	24	41'39.424	**1'33.351**	260,4	11 1'42.869
15	66	A. **HOFMANN**	GER	Kawasaki Racing	Kawasaki ZX-7RR	24	41'42.338	**1'36.265**	266,2	22 1'43.329
16	28	S. **FOTI**	ITA	Pedercini	Ducati 996 RS	23	40'20.497	**1 Lap**	261,0	18 1'43.802
17	5	M. **HECKLES**	GBR	Castrol Honda Rumi	Honda VTR 1000 SP2	23	40'45.645	**1 Lap**	254,2	6 1'43.751
18	36	I. **CLEMENTI**	ITA	Kawasaki Bertocchi	Kawasaki ZX-7RR	23	40'50.965	**1 Lap**	253,6	4 1'44.805
19	69	T. **MULOT**	FRA	White Endurance	Honda VTR 1000 SP1	23	40'53.367	**1 Lap**	252,4	4 1'45.614
					------Not Classified:------					
RET	33	J. **BORJA**	ESP	Spaziotel Racing	Ducati 998 RS	18	31'25.344	**6 Laps**	264,9	4 1'41.750
RET	6	P. **GODDARD**	AUS	Benelli Sport	Benelli Tornado 900	18	31'26.809	**6 Laps**	255,4	6 1'43.807
RET	100	N. **HODGSON**	GBR	HM Plant Ducati	Ducati 998 F 01	11	20'05.681	**13 Laps**	266,9	6 1'41.702
RET	23	J. **MRKYVKA**	CZE	JM Racing	Ducati 996 RS	9	16'23.872	**15 Laps**	256,7	4 1'46.097
RET	9	C. **WALKER**	GBR	Kawasaki Racing	Kawasaki ZX-7RR	0				

RACE 2

Laps 24 = 102,360 km - Avg. 152,926 km/h

	No.	Rider	Nat	Team	Bike	Laps	Time	Gap	Speed	Fastest Lap
1	1	T. **BAYLISS**	AUS	Ducati Infostrada	Ducati 998 F 02	24	40'09.633		266,2	20 1'39.701
2	2	C. **EDWARDS**	USA	Castrol Honda	Honda VTR 1000 SP2	24	40'11.283	**1.650**	270,2	21 1'39.808
3	11	R. **XAUS**	ESP	Ducati Infostrada	Ducati 998 F 02	24	40'14.698	**5.065**	268,2	7 1'39.679
4	155	B. **BOSTROM**	USA	Ducati L & M	Ducati 998 F 02	24	40'23.596	**13.963**	280,8	6 1'40.239
5	41	N. **HAGA**	JPN	Playstation2-FGF Aprilia	Aprilia RSV 1000	24	40'29.665	**20.032**	277,2	13 1'40.457
6	7	P. **CHILI**	ITA	Ducati NCR Axo	Ducati 998 RS	24	40'38.599	**28.966**	268,2	5 1'40.773
7	52	J. **TOSELAND**	GBR	HM Plant Ducati	Ducati 998 F 01	24	40'41.013	**31.380**	265,5	22 1'41.129
8	100	N. **HODGSON**	GBR	HM Plant Ducati	Ducati 998 F 01	24	40'47.976	**38.343**	270,9	2 1'40.769
9	9	C. **WALKER**	GBR	Kawasaki Racing	Kawasaki ZX-7RR	24	41'03.885	**54.252**	261,7	8 1'41.776
10	19	L. **PEDERCINI**	ITA	Pedercini	Ducati 998 RS	24	41'12.154	**1'02.521**	262,3	24 1'42.040
11	99	S. **MARTIN**	AUS	DFX Racing Ducati Pirelli	Ducati 998 RS	24	41'12.428	**1'02.795**	270,2	20 1'41.409
12	20	M. **BORCIANI**	ITA	Pedercini	Ducati 998 RS	24	41'13.843	**1'04.210**	268,2	19 1'41.923
13	66	A. **HOFMANN**	GER	Kawasaki Racing	Kawasaki ZX-7RR	24	41'29.370	**1'19.737**	264,9	5 1'42.971
14	46	M. **SANCHINI**	ITA	Kawasaki Bertocchi	Kawasaki ZX-7RR	24	41'33.398	**1'23.765**	260,4	4 1'42.835
15	6	P. **GODDARD**	AUS	Benelli Sport	Benelli Tornado 900	24	41'33.958	**1'24.325**	257,3	17 1'43.139
16	28	S. **FOTI**	ITA	Pedercini	Ducati 996 RS	24	41'45.381	**1'35.748**	260,4	10 1'43.208
17	5	M. **HECKLES**	GBR	Castrol Honda Rumi	Honda VTR 1000 SP2	24	41'51.207	**1'41.574**	253,6	10 1'43.522
					------Not Classified:------					
RET	30	A. **ANTONELLO**	ITA	DFX Racing Ducati Pirelli	Ducati 998 RS	19	32'42.196	**5 Laps**	268,9	19 1'41.821
RET	12	B. **PARKES**	AUS	Ducati NCR Parmalat	Ducati 998 RS	19	33'09.105	**5 Laps**	258,5	16 1'42.788
RET	33	J. **BORJA**	ESP	Spaziotel Racing	Ducati 998 RS	14	25'37.756	**10 Laps**	264,9	5 1'41.487
RET	36	I. **CLEMENTI**	ITA	Kawasaki Bertocchi	Kawasaki ZX-7RR	8	14'09.608	**16 Laps**	256,7	4 1'43.595
RET	69	T. **MULOT**	FRA	White Endurance	Honda VTR 1000 SP1	7	12'43.631	**17 Laps**	250,7	6 1'45.778
RET	10	G. **LAVILLA**	ESP	Alstare Suzuki Corona	Suzuki GSX-R750 Y	1	1'48.341	**23 Laps**	256,7	
NS	23	J. **MRKYVKA**	CZE	JM Racing	Ducati 996 RS					

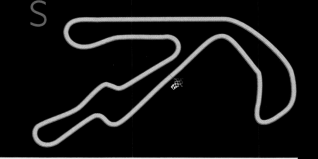

results

MISANO - RSM
21-22-23 June, 2002

RACE 1

Laps 25 = 101,500 km - Avg. 151,934 km/h

	No.	Rider	Nat	Team	Bike	Laps	Time	Gap	Speed	Fastest Lap
1	1	T. BAYLISS	AUS	Ducati Infostrada	Ducati 998 F 02	25	40'04.994		278,7	2 1'34.913
2	2	C. EDWARDS	USA	Castrol Honda	Honda VTR 1000 SP2	25	40'07.900	2.906	279,4	2 1'35.293
3	100	N. HODGSON	GBR	HM Plant Ducati	Ducati 998 F 01	25	40'19.089	14.095	279,4	2 1'35.319
4	41	N. HAGA	JPN	Playstation2-FGF Aprilia	Aprilia RSV 1000	25	40'23.994	19.000	273,8	2 1'35.849
5	155	B. BOSTROM	USA	Ducati L & M	Ducati 998 F 02	25	40'38.638	33.644	283,1	2 1'35.600
6	7	P. CHILI	ITA	Ducati NCR Axo	Ducati 998 RS	25	40'47.269	42.275	274,5	2 1'36.674
7	9	C. WALKER	GBR	Kawasaki Racing	Kawasaki ZX-7RR	25	40'52.893	47.899	271,0	2 1'36.700
8	52	J. TOSELAND	GBR	HM Plant Ducati	Ducati 998 F 01	25	40'54.879	49.885	272,4	4 1'36.934
9	19	L. PEDERCINI	ITA	Pedercini	Ducati 998 RS	25	40'58.539	53.545	273,1	2 1'36.999
10	10	G. LAVILLA	ESP	Alstare Suzuki Corona	Suzuki GSX-R750 Y	25	41'02.198	57.204	269,0	3 1'37.695
11	20	M. BORCIANI	ITA	Pedercini	Ducati 998 RS	25	41'08.065	1'03.071	273,8	4 1'37.108
12	46	M. SANCHINI	ITA	Kawasaki Bertocchi	Kawasaki ZX-7RR	25	41'15.067	1'10.073	265,1	2 1'37.523
13	99	S. MARTIN	AUS	DFX Racing Ducati Pirelli	Ducati 998 RS	25	41'20.220	1'15.226	273,8	3 1'38.080
14	28	S. FOTI	ITA	Pedercini	Ducati 996 RS	25	41'31.298	1'26.304	267,0	4 1'38.465
15	6	P. GODDARD	AUS	Benelli Sport	Benelli Tornado 900	25	41'38.214	1'33.220	265,1	7 1'39.234
16	113	P. BLORA	ITA	Pacific	Ducati 996 RS	24	40'05.751	1 Lap	266,4	4 1'38.823
17	36	I. CLEMENTI	ITA	Kawasaki Bertocchi	Kawasaki ZX-7RR	24	40'11.251	1 Lap	262,5	2 1'38.544
18	50	A. VALIA	ITA	Ass. Sportiva Bassani	Ducati 996 RS	24	40'34.026	1 Lap	267,7	3 1'39.771
19	5	M. HECKLES	GBR	Castrol Honda Rumi	Honda VTR 1000 SP2	24	40'57.278	1 Lap	261,8	11 1'40.379
20	68	B. STEY	FRA	White Endurance	Honda VTR 1000 SP1	24	40'57.348	1 Lap	256,3	6 1'40.620
21	61	M. MALEC	SLO	Magnat Auto	Ducati 996 RS	24	41'15.183	1 Lap	263,8	2 1'40.944
					Not Classified:					
RET	151	M. MALATESTA	ITA	Pro.Con.	Ducati 996 RS	5	8'42.539	20 Laps	268,3	3 1'39.418
RET	12	B. PARKES	AUS	Ducati NCR Parmalat	Ducati 998 RS	4	6'44.324	21 Laps	261,8	3 1'38.949
RET	40	G. SARTONI	ITA	Vemar Giesse	Ducati 996 RS	4	6'58.623	21 Laps	263,1	3 1'41.783
RET	11	R. XAUS	ESP	Ducati Infostrada	Ducati 998 F 02	3	4'51.671	22 Laps	281,6	3 1'35.585
RET	33	J. BORJA	ESP	Spaziotel Racing	Ducati 998 RS	3	4'58.841	22 Laps	267,0	2 1'37.536
RET	30	A. ANTONELLO	ITA	DFX Racing Ducati Pirelli	Ducati 998 RS	0			251,5	

RACE 2

Laps 25 = 101,500 km - Avg. 151,769 km/h

	No.	Rider	Nat	Team	Bike	Laps	Time	Gap	Speed	Fastest Lap
1	1	T. BAYLISS	AUS	Ducati Infostrada	Ducati 998 F 02	25	40'07.599		285,3	7 1'35.459
2	2	C. EDWARDS	USA	Castrol Honda	Honda VTR 1000 SP2	25	40'10.928	3.329	278,7	5 1'35.451
3	41	N. HAGA	JPN	Playstation2-FGF Aprilia	Aprilia RSV 1000	25	40'16.046	8.447	274,5	4 1'35.643
4	100	N. HODGSON	GBR	HM Plant Ducati	Ducati 998 F 01	25	40'21.688	14.089	279,4	3 1'35.547
5	155	B. BOSTROM	USA	Ducati L & M	Ducati 998 F 02	25	40'29.083	21.484	278,7	3 1'35.757
6	10	G. LAVILLA	ESP	Alstare Suzuki Corona	Suzuki GSX-R750 Y	25	40'43.765	36.166	279,4	2 1'36.410
7	7	P. CHILI	ITA	Ducati NCR Axo	Ducati 998 RS	25	40'44.143	36.544	274,5	3 1'36.215
8	9	C. WALKER	GBR	Kawasaki Racing	Kawasaki ZX-7RR	25	40'52.365	44.766	269,0	4 1'36.862
9	19	L. PEDERCINI	ITA	Pedercini	Ducati 998 RS	25	41'07.851	1'00.252	273,1	2 1'36.987
10	20	M. BORCIANI	ITA	Pedercini	Ducati 998 RS	25	41'14.117	1'06.518	275,2	7 1'37.710
11	46	M. SANCHINI	ITA	Kawasaki Bertocchi	Kawasaki ZX-7RR	25	41'22.150	1'14.551	265,1	2 1'37.908
12	99	S. MARTIN	AUS	DFX Racing Ducati Pirelli	Ducati 998 RS	25	41'23.937	1'16.338	274,5	8 1'38.264
13	151	M. MALATESTA	ITA	Pro.Con.	Ducati 996 RS	25	41'32.894	1'25.295	269,0	5 1'38.564
14	12	B. PARKES	AUS	Ducati NCR Parmalat	Ducati 998 RS	25	41'35.667	1'28.068	265,7	6 1'38.763
15	68	B. STEY	FRA	White Endurance	Honda VTR 1000 SP1	24	40'58.997	1 Lap	258,7	6 1'40.308
16	61	M. MALEC	SLO	Magnat Auto	Ducati 996 RS	24	41'20.484	1 Lap	261,2	4 1'41.010
17	40	G. SARTONI	ITA	Vemar Giesse	Ducati 996 RS	24	41'27.880	1 Lap	268,3	12 1'41.635
					Not Classified:					
RET	6	P. GODDARD	AUS	Benelli Sport	Benelli Tornado 900	15	24'49.329	10 Laps	264,4	5 1'38.442
RET	36	I. CLEMENTI	ITA	Kawasaki Bertocchi	Kawasaki ZX-7RR	14	23'16.077	11 Laps	261,8	3 1'38.491
RET	113	P. BLORA	ITA	Pacific	Ducati 996 RS	10	16'45.508	15 Laps	265,1	9 1'39.499
RET	5	M. HECKLES	GBR	Castrol Honda Rumi	Honda VTR 1000 SP2	8	13'33.600	17 Laps	263,1	6 1'40.127
RET	28	S. FOTI	ITA	Pedercini	Ducati 996 RS	6	10'01.221	19 Laps	257,5	6 1'38.693
RET	11	R. XAUS	ESP	Ducati Infostrada	Ducati 998 F 02	5	8'05.922	20 Laps	274,5	2 1'36.035
RET	52	J. TOSELAND	GBR	HM Plant Ducati	Ducati 998 F 01	4	6'33.372	21 Laps	266,4	4 1'36.884
RET	30	A. ANTONELLO	ITA	DFX Racing Ducati Pirelli	Ducati 998 RS	2	3'22.439	23 Laps	272,4	2 1'37.720
RET	33	J. BORJA	ESP	Spaziotel Racing	Ducati 998 RS	2	3'23.134	23 Laps	267,0	2 1'38.754
RET	50	A. VALIA	ITA	Ass. Sportiva Bassani	Ducati 996 RS	0				

LAGUNA SECA - USA
12-13-14 July, 2002

S U P E R B I K E

RACE 1

Laps 28 = 101,080 km - Avg. 150,433 km/h

	No.	Rider	Nat	Team	Bike	Laps	Time	Gap	Speed	Fastest Lap
1	1	T. **BAYLISS**	AUS	Ducati Infostrada	Ducati 998 F 02	28	40'18.943		246,2	5 1'25.657
2	11	R. **XAUS**	ESP	Ducati Infostrada	Ducati 998 F 02	28	40'19.282	**0.339**	244,7	6 1'25.727
3	2	C. **EDWARDS**	USA	Castrol Honda	Honda VTR 1000 SP2	28	40'20.994	**2.051**	245,1	6 1'25.776
4	69	N. **HAYDEN**	USA	American Honda	Honda RC51	28	40'21.531	**2.588**	246,2	4 1'25.722
5	100	N. **HODGSON**	GBR	HM Plant Ducati	Ducati 998 F 01	28	40'23.047	**4.104**	245,8	4 1'25.783
6	32	E. **BOSTROM**	USA	Kawasaki Racing	Kawasaki ZX-7RR	28	40'30.677	**11.734**	250,3	5 1'26.093
7	120	A. **YATES**	USA	Yoshimura Suzuki	Suzuki GSX-R750 Y	28	40'36.604	**17.661**	248,0	5 1'26.082
8	155	B. **BOSTROM**	USA	Ducati L & M	Ducati 998 F 02	28	40'42.695	**23.752**	250,7	6 1'25.999
9	52	J. **TOSELAND**	GBR	HM Plant Ducati	Ducati 998 F 01	28	40'45.380	**26.437**	245,8	5 1'26.147
10	101	M. **MLADIN**	AUS	Yoshimura Suzuki	Suzuki GSX-R750 Y	28	40'49.142	**30.199**	246,5	4 1'26.477
11	9	C. **WALKER**	GBR	Kawasaki Racing	Kawasaki ZX-7RR	28	40'59.888	**40.945**	238,9	11 1'27.189
12	7	P. **CHILI**	ITA	Ducati NCR Axo	Ducati 998 RS	28	40'59.950	**41.007**	240,4	12 1'27.031
13	110	D. **CHANDLER**	USA	HMC Ducati Racing	Ducati 998 R	28	41'02.140	**43.197**	242,5	14 1'27.118
14	99	S. **MARTIN**	AUS	DFX Racing Ducati Pirelli	Ducati 998 RS	28	41'15.619	**56.676**	241,1	4 1'27.494
15	12	B. **PARKES**	AUS	Ducati NCR Parmalat	Ducati 998 RS	28	41'25.973	**1'07.030**	246,2	6 1'28.002
16	6	P. **GODDARD**	AUS	Benelli Sport	Benelli Tornado 900	28	41'33.213	**1'14.270**	235,1	6 1'28.123
17	19	L. **PEDERCINI**	ITA	Pedercini	Ducati 998 RS	28	41'33.567	**1'14.624**	238,6	12 1'27.713
18	30	A. **ANTONELLO**	ITA	DFX Racing Ducati Pirelli	Ducati 998 RS	28	41'38.835	**1'19.892**	239,3	10 1'28.482
19	46	M. **SANCHINI**	ITA	Kawasaki Bertocchi	Kawasaki ZX-7RR	28	41'42.700	**1'23.757**	232,1	14 1'28.485
20	5	M. **HECKLES**	GBR	Castrol Honda Rumi	Honda VTR 1000 SP2	27	40'45.350	**1 Lap**	230,2	21 1'29.458
21	72	M. **MILLER**	USA	White Endurance	Honda VTR 1000 SP1	27	41'04.870	**1 Lap**	229,5	23 1'29.963
22	68	B. **STEY**	FRA	White Endurance	Honda VTR 1000 SP1	27	41'09.892	**1 Lap**	232,8	5 1'29.896

--Not Classified:--

	No.	Rider	Nat	Team	Bike	Laps	Time	Gap	Speed	Fastest Lap
RET	36	I. **CLEMENTI**	ITA	Kawasaki Bertocchi	Kawasaki ZX-7RR	20	29'52.044	**8 Laps**	234,5	14 1'28.659
RET	28	S. **FOTI**	ITA	Pedercini	Ducati 996 RS	17	25'25.329	**11 Laps**	239,3	14 1'28.493
RET	41	N. **HAGA**	JPN	Playstation2-FGF Aprilia	Aprilia RSV 1000	14	20'39.141	**14 Laps**	249,2	4 1'25.475
RET	20	M. **BORCIANI**	ITA	Pedercini	Ducati 998 RS	9	18'14.343	**19 Laps**	236,5	3 1'28.466

RACE 2

Laps 28 = 101,080 km - Avg. 150,691 km/h

	No.	Rider	Nat	Team	Bike	Laps	Time	Gap	Speed	Fastest Lap
1	2	C. **EDWARDS**	USA	Castrol Honda	Honda VTR 1000 SP2	28	40'14.793		245,1	5 1'25.688
2	1	T. **BAYLISS**	AUS	Ducati Infostrada	Ducati 998 F 02	28	40'15.879	**1.086**	247,7	7 1'25.623
3	100	N. **HODGSON**	GBR	HM Plant Ducati	Ducati 998 F 01	28	40'16.465	**1.672**	245,8	15 1'25.597
4	32	E. **BOSTROM**	USA	Kawasaki Racing	Kawasaki ZX-7RR	28	40'19.836	**5.043**	250,7	12 1'25.814
5	155	B. **BOSTROM**	USA	Ducati L & M	Ducati 998 F 02	28	40'26.636	**11.843**	245,8	9 1'25.739
6	52	J. **TOSELAND**	GBR	HM Plant Ducati	Ducati 998 F 01	28	40'40.540	**25.747**	245,1	6 1'26.442
7	7	P. **CHILI**	ITA	Ducati NCR Axo	Ducati 998 RS	28	40'41.365	**26.572**	244,0	6 1'26.419
8	120	A. **YATES**	USA	Yoshimura Suzuki	Suzuki GSX-R750 Y	28	40'45.027	**30.234**	245,4	23 1'26.564
9	110	D. **CHANDLER**	USA	HMC Ducati Racing	Ducati 998 R	28	40'54.137	**39.344**	241,1	24 1'26.800
10	9	C. **WALKER**	GBR	Kawasaki Racing	Kawasaki ZX-7RR	28	41'02.466	**47.673**	236,5	4 1'26.906
11	99	S. **MARTIN**	AUS	DFX Racing Ducati Pirelli	Ducati 998 RS	28	41'10.256	**55.463**	239,3	7 1'27.532
12	12	B. **PARKES**	AUS	Ducati NCR Parmalat	Ducati 998 RS	28	41'13.858	**59.065**	246,5	6 1'27.474
13	69	N. **HAYDEN**	USA	American Honda	Honda RC51	28	41'21.789	**1'06.996**	246,2	9 1'25.791
14	6	P. **GODDARD**	AUS	Benelli Sport	Benelli Tornado 900	28	41'29.634	**1'14.841**	233,8	4 1'28.255
15	46	M. **SANCHINI**	ITA	Kawasaki Bertocchi	Kawasaki ZX-7RR	28	41'33.856	**1'19.063**	234,5	7 1'28.092
16	19	L. **PEDERCINI**	ITA	Pedercini	Ducati 998 RS	28	41'37.660	**1'22.867**	241,8	7 1'27.570
17	28	S. **FOTI**	ITA	Pedercini	Ducati 996 RS	28	41'38.149	**1'23.356**	237,2	17 1'28.152
18	20	M. **BORCIANI**	ITA	Pedercini	Ducati 998 RS	28	41'39.173	**1'24.380**	236,9	6 1'28.036
19	11	R. **XAUS**	ESP	Ducati Infostrada	Ducati 998 F 02	27	40'26.969	**1 Lap**	244,0	18 1'25.974
20	5	M. **HECKLES**	GBR	Castrol Honda Rumi	Honda VTR 1000 SP2	27	40'27.375	**1 Lap**	229,2	11 1'28.812
21	36	I. **CLEMENTI**	ITA	Kawasaki Bertocchi	Kawasaki ZX-7RR	27	40'38.545	**1 Lap**	232,5	6 1'28.961
22	72	M. **MILLER**	USA	White Endurance	Honda VTR 1000 SP1	27	40'58.398	**1 Lap**	231,5	22 1'29.779
23	68	B. **STEY**	FRA	White Endurance	Honda VTR 1000 SP1	27	41'08.544	**1 Lap**	232,5	11 1'30.070

--Not Classified:--

	No.	Rider	Nat	Team	Bike	Laps	Time	Gap	Speed	Fastest Lap
RET	101	M. **MLADIN**	AUS	Yoshimura Suzuki	Suzuki GSX-R750 Y	14	20'39.517	**14 Laps**	245,8	3 1'26.522
RET	41	N. **HAGA**	JPN	Playstation2-FGF Aprilia	Aprilia RSV 1000	13	18'45.801	**15 Laps**	247,3	4 1'25.716
RET	30	A. **ANTONELLO**	ITA	DFX Racing Ducati Pirelli	Ducati 998 RS	3	4'36.598	**25 Laps**	240,4	2 1'29.622

BRANDS HATCH - GBR

26-27-28 July, 2002

RACE 1

Laps 25 = 105,525 km - Avg. 173,660 km/h

	No.	Rider	Nat	Team	Bike	Laps	Time	Gap	Speed	Fastest Lap
1	2	C. EDWARDS	USA	Castrol Honda	Honda VTR 1000 SP2	25	36'27.555		267,0	11 1'26.758
2	100	N. HODGSON	GBR	HM Plant Ducati	Ducati 998 F 01	25	36'28.728	1.173	265,7	9 1'26.880
3	1	T. BAYLISS	AUS	Ducati Infostrada	Ducati 998 F 02	25	36'37.882	10.327	269,6	11 1'26.690
4	41	N. HAGA	JPN	Playstation2-FGF Aprilia	Aprilia RSV 1000	25	36'49.798	22.243	269,6	6 1'27.670
5	11	R. XAUS	ESP	Ducati Infostrada	Ducati 998 F 02	25	36'50.038	22.483	267,0	2 1'27.630
6	9	C. WALKER	GBR	Kawasaki Racing	Kawasaki ZX-7RR	25	36'54.051	26.496	260,7	14 1'27.776
7	155	B. BOSTROM	USA	Ducati L & M	Ducati 998 F 02	25	36'54.090	26.535	257,0	11 1'27.735
8	7	P. CHILI	ITA	Ducati NCR Axo	Ducati 998 RS	25	36'54.343	26.788	267,6	18 1'27.872
9	52	J. TOSELAND	GBR	HM Plant Ducati	Ducati 998 F 01	25	36'59.877	32.322	260,7	2 1'28.081
10	55	S. BYRNE	GBR	Renegade Ducati	Ducati 998 RS	25	37'00.189	32.634	257,6	24 1'28.005
11	33	J. BORJA	ESP	Spaziotel Racing	Ducati 998 RS	25	37'05.747	38.192	265,0	8 1'27.961
12	30	A. ANTONELLO	ITA	DFX Racing Ducati Pirelli	Ducati 998 RS	25	37'14.510	46.955	264,4	19 1'28.547
13	14	H. IZUTSU	JPN	Kawasaki Racing	Kawasaki ZX-7RR	25	37'14.802	47.247	260,0	19 1'28.372
14	56	D. ELLISON	GBR	D & B Racing	Ducati 996 RS	25	37'16.340	48.785	262,5	25 1'28.230
15	10	G. LAVILLA	ESP	Alstare Suzuki Corona	Suzuki GSX-R750 Y	25	37'17.445	49.890	257,0	2 1'28.184
16	20	M. BORCIANI	ITA	Pedercini	Ducati 998 RS	25	37'25.207	57.652	265,7	11 1'28.880
17	5	M. HECKLES	GBR	Castrol Honda Rumi	Honda VTR 1000 SP2	25	37'35.097	1'07.542	255,2	7 1'29.093
18	6	P. GODDARD	AUS	Benelli Sport	Benelli Tornado 900	25	37'35.784	1'08.229	254,7	4 1'29.455
19	99	S. MARTIN	AUS	DFX Racing Ducati Pirelli	Ducati 998 RS	25	37'48.858	1'21.303	264,4	12 1'28.741
20	57	G. RICHARDS	GBR	Hawk Kawasaki	Kawasaki ZX-7RR	25	37'52.675	1'25.120	254,7	4 1'28.673

--Not Classified:--

	No.	Rider	Nat	Team	Bike	Laps	Time	Gap	Speed	Fastest Lap
RET	54	M. RUTTER	GBR	Renegade Ducati	Ducati 998 RS	20	31'40.219	5 Laps	261,3	9 1'27.720
RET	46	M. SANCHINI	ITA	Kawasaki Bertocchi	Kawasaki ZX-7RR	12	18'02.729	13 Laps	248,9	11 1'28.833
RET	12	B. PARKES	AUS	Ducati NCR Parmalat	Ducati 998 RS	8	12'10.860	17 Laps	247,2	4 1'29.335
RET	19	L. PEDERCINI	ITA	Pedercini	Ducati 998 RS	6	9'18.240	19 Laps	252,3	2 1'30.415
RET	68	B. STEY	FRA	White Endurance	Honda VTR 1000 SP1	4	6'13.860	21 Laps	245,1	2 1'30.664
RET	36	I. CLEMENTI	ITA	Kawasaki Bertocchi	Kawasaki ZX-7RR	3	4'42.826	22 Laps	246,1	2 1'29.727

RACE 2

Laps 25 = 105,525 km - Avg. 173,652 km/h

	No.	Rider	Nat	Team	Bike	Laps	Time	Gap	Speed	Fastest Lap
1	2	C. EDWARDS	USA	Castrol Honda	Honda VTR 1000 SP2	25	36'27.655		266,3	9 1'26.711
2	1	T. BAYLISS	AUS	Ducati Infostrada	Ducati 998 F 02	25	36'29.981	2.326	271,5	5 1'26.855
3	100	N. HODGSON	GBR	HM Plant Ducati	Ducati 998 F 01	25	36'30.403	2.748	264,4	10 1'26.940
4	155	B. BOSTROM	USA	Ducati L & M	Ducati 998 F 02	25	36'40.785	13.130	259,4	14 1'27.194
5	41	N. HAGA	JPN	Playstation2-FGF Aprilia	Aprilia RSV 1000	25	36'40.927	13.272	269,6	15 1'27.260
6	11	R. XAUS	ESP	Ducati Infostrada	Ducati 998 F 02	25	36'40.948	13.293	268,9	5 1'26.889
7	7	P. CHILI	ITA	Ducati NCR Axo	Ducati 998 RS	25	36'42.619	14.964	267,6	6 1'26.872
8	9	C. WALKER	GBR	Kawasaki Racing	Kawasaki ZX-7RR	25	36'49.579	21.924	260,7	4 1'27.536
9	54	M. RUTTER	GBR	Renegade Ducati	Ducati 998 RS	25	36'52.363	24.708	259,4	3 1'27.406
10	55	S. BYRNE	GBR	Renegade Ducati	Ducati 998 RS	25	36'57.485	29.830	258,8	11 1'27.729
11	33	J. BORJA	ESP	Spaziotel Racing	Ducati 998 RS	25	36'57.871	30.216	265,0	10 1'27.778
12	10	G. LAVILLA	ESP	Alstare Suzuki Corona	Suzuki GSX-R750 Y	25	36'58.264	30.609	259,4	10 1'27.768
13	30	A. ANTONELLO	ITA	DFX Racing Ducati Pirelli	Ducati 998 RS	25	37'12.025	44.370	263,1	11 1'28.389
14	57	G. RICHARDS	GBR	Hawk Kawasaki	Kawasaki ZX-7RR	25	37'14.449	46.794	255,8	5 1'28.270
15	20	M. BORCIANI	ITA	Pedercini	Ducati 998 RS	25	37'19.286	51.631	264,4	7 1'28.563
16	99	S. MARTIN	AUS	DFX Racing Ducati Pirelli	Ducati 998 RS	25	37'22.034	54.379	261,3	11 1'28.629
17	14	H. IZUTSU	JPN	Kawasaki Racing	Kawasaki ZX-7RR	25	37'25.808	58.153	255,2	6 1'28.599
18	12	B. PARKES	AUS	Ducati NCR Parmalat	Ducati 998 RS	25	37'32.699	1'05.044	249,5	7 1'29.243
19	46	M. SANCHINI	ITA	Kawasaki Bertocchi	Kawasaki ZX-7RR	25	37'33.638	1'05.983	248,4	7 1'29.311
20	5	M. HECKLES	GBR	Castrol Honda Rumi	Honda VTR 1000 SP2	25	37'36.488	1'08.833	252,9	6 1'29.086
21	36	I. CLEMENTI	ITA	Kawasaki Bertocchi	Kawasaki ZX-7RR	25	37'41.682	1'14.027	247,8	5 1'29.225

--Not Classified:--

	No.	Rider	Nat	Team	Bike	Laps	Time	Gap	Speed	Fastest Lap
RET	56	D. ELLISON	GBR	D & B Racing	Ducati 996 RS	24	35'42.090	1 Lap	263,8	14 1'28.105
RET	52	J. TOSELAND	GBR	HM Plant Ducati	Ducati 998 F 01	14	20'43.167	11 Laps	258,2	11 1'27.770
RET	19	L. PEDERCINI	ITA	Pedercini	Ducati 998 RS	3	4'41.625	22 Laps	251,2	3 1'30.182
RET	68	B. STEY	FRA	White Endurance	Honda VTR 1000 SP1	3	4'43.559	22 Laps	241,8	2 1'30.999
RET	6	P. GODDARD	AUS	Benelli Sport	Benelli Tornado 900	0				

OSCHERSLEBEN – GER
30-31 August - 1 September, 2002

RACE 1

Laps 28 = 102,676 km - Avg. 150,518 km/h

	No.	Rider	Nat	Team	Bike	Laps	Time	Gap	Speed	Fastest Lap
1	2	C. EDWARDS	USA	Castrol Honda	Honda VTR 1000 SP2	28	40'55.744		263,6	5 1'27.007
2	1	T. BAYLISS	AUS	Ducati Infostrada	Ducati 998 F 02	28	40'57.485	1.741	265,5	11 1'27.149
3	100	N. HODGSON	GBR	HM Plant Ducati	Ducati 998 F 01	28	41'00.061	4.317	265,5	10 1'27.251
4	155	B. BOSTROM	USA	Ducati L & M	Ducati 998 F 02	28	41'19.459	23.715	259,8	3 1'27.497
5	7	P. CHILI	ITA	Ducati NCR Axo	Ducati 998 RS	28	41'22.267	26.523	268,2	5 1'27.503
6	52	J. TOSELAND	GBR	HM Plant Ducati	Ducati 998 F 01	28	41'25.972	30.228	267,5	7 1'28.047
7	41	N. HAGA	JPN	Playstation2-FGF Aprilia	Aprilia RSV 1000	28	41'26.102	30.358	257,9	4 1'27.886
8	10	G. LAVILLA	ESP	Alstare Suzuki Corona	Suzuki GSX-R750 Y	28	41'38.270	42.526	257,3	18 1'28.446
9	9	C. WALKER	GBR	Kawasaki Racing	Kawasaki ZX-7RR	28	41'38.471	42.727	255,4	4 1'28.129
10	12	B. PARKES	AUS	Ducati NCR Parmalat	Ducati 998 RS	28	41'44.577	48.833	256,7	13 1'28.704
11	14	H. IZUTSU	JPN	Kawasaki Racing	Kawasaki ZX-7RR	28	41'55.125	59.381	259,1	12 1'28.749
12	6	P. GODDARD	AUS	Benelli Sport	Benelli Tornado 900	28	42'17.845	1'22.101	257,9	14 1'29.877
13	19	L. PEDERCINI	ITA	Pedercini	Ducati 998 RS	28	42'20.777	1'25.033	251,8	9 1'29.542
14	28	S. FOTI	ITA	Pedercini	Ducati 996 RS	28	42'25.824	1'30.080	256,0	16 1'30.078
15	5	M. HECKLES	GBR	Castrol Honda Rumi	Honda VTR 1000 SP2	27	41'11.836	1 Lap	244,4	15 1'30.477
16	46	M. SANCHINI	ITA	Kawasaki Bertocchi	Kawasaki ZX-7RR	27	41'20.843	1 Lap	243,8	4 1'30.167
17	70	Y. GYGER	SUI	White Endurance	Honda VTR 1000 SP1	27	41'59.838	1 Lap	234,2	17 1'31.654
18	69	T. MULOT	FRA	Pacific	Ducati 996 SPS	27	42'09.576	1 Lap	247,8	20 1'32.687

---Not Classified:---

	No.	Rider	Nat	Team	Bike	Laps	Time	Gap	Speed	Fastest Lap
RET	36	I. CLEMENTI	ITA	Kawasaki Bertocchi	Kawasaki ZX-7RR	25	38'30.458	3 Laps	241,1	20 1'30.582
RET	11	R. XAUS	ESP	Ducati Infostrada	Ducati 998 F 02	22	32'12.840	6 Laps	267,5	10 1'27.248
RET	20	M. BORCIANI	ITA	Pedercini	Ducati 998 RS	21	31'40.964	7 Laps	253,6	9 1'29.478
RET	23	J. MRKYVKA	CZE	JM Racing	Ducati 996 RS	7	11'02.158	21 Laps	234,7	7 1'33.042
RET	30	A. ANTONELLO	ITA	DFX Racing Ducati Pirelli	Ducati 998 RS	0				

RACE 2

Laps 28 = 102,676 km - Avg. 150,458 km/h

	No.	Rider	Nat	Team	Bike	Laps	Time	Gap	Speed	Fastest Lap
1	2	C. EDWARDS	USA	Castrol Honda	Honda VTR 1000 SP2	28	40'56.724		261,7	5 1'26.549
2	1	T. BAYLISS	AUS	Ducati Infostrada	Ducati 998 F 02	28	41'00.585	3.861	264,9	4 1'27.059
3	100	N. HODGSON	GBR	HM Plant Ducati	Ducati 998 F 01	28	41'03.747	7.023	267,5	6 1'27.162
4	41	N. HAGA	JPN	Playstation2-FGF Aprilia	Aprilia RSV 1000	28	41'05.021	8.297	257,9	6 1'27.209
5	11	R. XAUS	ESP	Ducati Infostrada	Ducati 998 F 02	28	41'08.899	12.175	262,3	12 1'27.511
6	155	B. BOSTROM	USA	Ducati L & M	Ducati 998 F 02	28	41'22.873	26.149	259,1	6 1'27.512
7	7	P. CHILI	ITA	Ducati NCR Axo	Ducati 998 RS	28	41'27.869	31.145	266,9	2 1'27.538
8	52	J. TOSELAND	GBR	HM Plant Ducati	Ducati 998 F 01	28	41'29.115	32.391	250,7	6 1'28.112
9	10	G. LAVILLA	ESP	Alstare Suzuki Corona	Suzuki GSX-R750 Y	28	41'42.001	45.277	261,7	5 1'28.122
10	12	B. PARKES	AUS	Ducati NCR Parmalat	Ducati 998 RS	28	41'58.510	1'01.786	250,1	12 1'29.071
11	20	M. BORCIANI	ITA	Pedercini	Ducati 998 RS	28	42'11.508	1'14.784	256,0	12 1'29.147
12	19	L. PEDERCINI	ITA	Pedercini	Ducati 998 RS	28	42'16.236	1'19.512	253,6	5 1'29.280
13	36	I. CLEMENTI	ITA	Kawasaki Bertocchi	Kawasaki ZX-7RR	28	42'26.530	1'29.806	241,6	6 1'29.850
14	46	M. SANCHINI	ITA	Kawasaki Bertocchi	Kawasaki ZX-7RR	27	41'12.177	1 Lap	244,4	5 1'30.333
15	9	C. WALKER	GBR	Kawasaki Racing	Kawasaki ZX-7RR	27	41'21.510	1 Lap	250,7	6 1'28.243
16	5	M. HECKLES	GBR	Castrol Honda Rumi	Honda VTR 1000 SP2	27	41'43.573	1 Lap	245,5	11 1'31.360
17	69	T. MULOT	FRA	Pacific	Ducati 996 SPS	27	42'08.354	1 Lap	241,1	4 1'31.954

---Not Classified:---

	No.	Rider	Nat	Team	Bike	Laps	Time	Gap	Speed	Fastest Lap
RET	28	S. FOTI	ITA	Pedercini	Ducati 996 RS	24	36'57.443	4 Laps	249,5	5 1'30.277
RET	6	P. GODDARD	AUS	Benelli Sport	Benelli Tornado 900	21	31'43.969	7 Laps	255,4	14 1'29.970
RET	14	H. IZUTSU	JPN	Kawasaki Racing	Kawasaki ZX-7RR	21	32'17.857	7 Laps	248,3	10 1'29.267
RET	23	J. MRKYVKA	CZE	JM Racing	Ducati 996 RS	9	14'18.590	19 Laps	241,6	3 1'32.324
RET	70	Y. GYGER	SUI	White Endurance	Honda VTR 1000 SP1	6	9'44.637	22 Laps	234,7	4 1'33.853
RET	30	A. ANTONELLO	ITA	DFX Racing Ducati Pirelli	Ducati 998 RS	2	3'24.052	26 Laps	243,8	2 1'45.706

ASSEN - NL
6-7-8 September, 2002

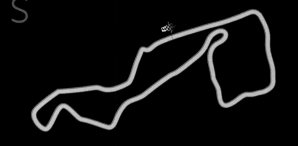

RACE 1

Laps 16 = 96,432 km - Avg. 175,455 km/h

	No.	Rider	Nat	Team	Bike	Laps	Time	Gap	Speed	Fastest Lap
1	2	C. EDWARDS	USA	Castrol Honda	Honda VTR 1000 SP2	16	32'58.601		264,1	5 2'02.395
2	1	T. BAYLISS	AUS	Ducati Infostrada	Ducati 998 F 02	16	33'02.207	3.606	260,9	13 2'02.760
3	41	N. HAGA	JPN	Playstation2-FGF Aprilia	Aprilia RSV 1000	16	33'03.952	5.351	248,3	7 2'03.241
4	11	R. XAUS	ESP	Ducati Infostrada	Ducati 998 F 02	16	33'06.342	7.741	252,9	2 2'02.962
5	7	P. CHILI	ITA	Ducati NCR Axo	Ducati 998 RS	16	33'14.863	16.262	255,3	6 2'03.205
6	52	J. TOSELAND	GBR	HM Plant Ducati	Ducati 998 F 01	16	33'18.193	19.592	242,7	15 2'04.017
7	10	G. LAVILLA	ESP	Alstare Suzuki Corona	Suzuki GSX-R750 Y	16	33'20.483	21.882	254,1	13 2'03.941
8	155	B. BOSTROM	USA	Ducati L & M	Ducati 998 F 02	16	33'20.767	22.166	239,5	6 2'04.147
9	12	B. PARKES	AUS	Ducati NCR Parmalat	Ducati 998 RS	16	33'35.075	36.474	248,8	3 2'04.564
10	33	J. BORJA	ESP	Spaziotel Racing	Ducati 998 RS	16	33'42.728	44.127	250,6	4 2'04.248
11	20	M. BORCIANI	ITA	Pedercini	Ducati 998 RS	16	33'45.237	46.636	244,3	3 2'05.224
12	6	P. GODDARD	AUS	Benelli Sport	Benelli Tornado 900	16	34'03.117	1'04.516	251,2	3 2'06.686
13	46	M. SANCHINI	ITA	Kawasaki Bertocchi	Kawasaki ZX-7RR	16	34'03.637	1'05.036	230,3	5 2'06.585
14	28	S. FOTI	ITA	Pedercini	Ducati 996 RS	16	34'37.457	1'38.856	234,8	4 2'07.657
15	60	J. VIDAL	ESP	White Endurance	Honda VTR 1000 SP1	16	34'49.714	1'51.113	222,7	5 2'08.849
16	69	T. MULOT	FRA	Pacific	Ducati 996 SPS	16	34'59.915	2'01.314	240,5	2 2'09.371
17	5	M. HECKLES	GBR	Castrol Honda Rumi	Honda VTR 1000 SP2	15	33'53.684	1 Lap	240,5	6 2'07.384
				------Not Classified:------						
RET	36	I. CLEMENTI	ITA	Kawasaki Bertocchi	Kawasaki ZX-7RR	13	27'40.906	3 Laps	246,6	2 2'06.123
RET	19	L. PEDERCINI	ITA	Pedercini	Ducati 998 RS	9	20'15.202	7 Laps	254,7	2 2'05.800
RET	99	S. MARTIN	AUS	DFX Racing Ducati Pirelli	Ducati 998 RS	7	23'53.160	9 Laps	225,5	6 2'09.337
RET	9	C. WALKER	GBR	Kawasaki Racing	Kawasaki ZX-7RR	6	12'34.759	10 Laps	240,5	4 2'04.403
RET	30	A. ANTONELLO	ITA	DFX Racing Ducati Pirelli	Ducati 998 RS	6	13'10.561	10 Laps	238,4	4 2'06.982
RET	100	N. HODGSON	GBR	HM Plant Ducati	Ducati 998 F 01	4	8'35.157	12 Laps	242,2	3 2'03.625

RACE 2

Laps 16 = 96,432 km - Avg. 175,341 km/h

	No.	Rider	Nat	Team	Bike	Laps	Time	Gap	Speed	Fastest Lap
1	2	C. EDWARDS	USA	Castrol Honda	Honda VTR 1000 SP2	16	32'59.881		264,7	3 2'02.657
2	7	P. CHILI	ITA	Ducati NCR Axo	Ducati 998 RS	16	33'07.387	7.506	252,9	2 2'02.945
3	52	J. TOSELAND	GBR	HM Plant Ducati	Ducati 998 F 01	16	33'10.923	11.042	246,0	2 2'03.579
4	100	N. HODGSON	GBR	HM Plant Ducati	Ducati 998 F 01	16	33'17.971	18.090	255,3	2 2'02.944
5	155	B. BOSTROM	USA	Ducati L & M	Ducati 998 F 02	16	33'23.576	23.695	243,2	4 2'04.093
6	41	N. HAGA	JPN	Playstation2-FGF Aprilia	Aprilia RSV 1000	16	33'24.137	24.256	254,7	3 2'03.053
7	9	C. WALKER	GBR	Kawasaki Racing	Kawasaki ZX-7RR	16	33'25.767	25.886	247,1	2 2'03.669
8	12	B. PARKES	AUS	Ducati NCR Parmalat	Ducati 998 RS	16	33'41.065	41.184	248,8	2 2'04.498
9	20	M. BORCIANI	ITA	Pedercini	Ducati 998 RS	16	33'49.938	50.057	247,7	2 2'05.058
10	19	L. PEDERCINI	ITA	Pedercini	Ducati 998 RS	16	33'55.935	56.054	254,7	2 2'05.601
11	6	P. GODDARD	AUS	Benelli Sport	Benelli Tornado 900	16	33'57.973	58.092	252,3	16 2'06.316
12	46	M. SANCHINI	ITA	Kawasaki Bertocchi	Kawasaki ZX-7RR	16	34'02.215	1'02.334	232,8	4 2'06.240
13	30	A. ANTONELLO	ITA	DFX Racing Ducati Pirelli	Ducati 998 RS	16	34'04.849	1'04.968	251,7	8 2'06.831
14	36	I. CLEMENTI	ITA	Kawasaki Bertocchi	Kawasaki ZX-7RR	16	34'05.363	1'05.482	251,7	4 2'06.873
15	5	M. HECKLES	GBR	Castrol Honda Rumi	Honda VTR 1000 SP2	16	34'13.405	1'13.524	242,7	8 2'06.725
16	28	S. FOTI	ITA	Pedercini	Ducati 996 RS	16	34'34.311	1'34.430	234,3	4 2'06.947
17	69	T. MULOT	FRA	Pacific	Ducati 996 SPS	16	34'55.959	1'56.078	238,4	6 2'09.831
				------Not Classified:------						
RET	1	T. BAYLISS	AUS	Ducati Infostrada	Ducati 998 F 02	9	18'38.139	7 Laps	257,8	2 2'02.704
RET	60	J. VIDAL	ESP	White Endurance	Honda VTR 1000 SP1	7	15'29.707	9 Laps	231,8	4 2'08.274
RET	11	R. XAUS	ESP	Ducati Infostrada	Ducati 998 F 02	6	18'11.428	10 Laps	247,1	2 2'02.502
RET	10	G. LAVILLA	ESP	Alstare Suzuki Corona	Suzuki GSX-R750 Y	5	11'39.054	11 Laps	245,5	3 2'03.996
RET	33	J. BORJA	ESP	Spaziotel Racing	Ducati 998 RS	1	2'11.568	15 Laps	231,8	

IMOLA - ITA
27-28-29 September, 2002

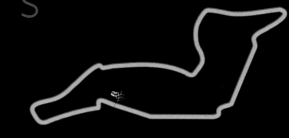

RACE 1

Laps 21 = 103,593 km - Avg. 162,334 km/h

	No.	Rider	Nat	Team	Bike	Laps	Time	Gap	Speed	Fastest Lap
1	2	C. EDWARDS	USA	Castrol Honda	Honda VTR 1000 SP2	21	38'17.324			17 1'48.717
2	1	T. BAYLISS	AUS	Ducati Infostrada	Ducati 998 F 02	21	38'17.838	0.514		5 1'48.759
3	11	R. XAUS	ESP	Ducati Infostrada	Ducati 998 F 02	21	38'25.975	8.651		18 1'49.063
4	100	N. HODGSON	GBR	HM Plant Ducati	Ducati 998 F 01	21	38'37.719	20.395		6 1'49.721
5	41	N. HAGA	JPN	Playstation2-FGF Aprilia	Aprilia RSV 1000	21	38'38.137	20.813		5 1'49.436
6	52	J. TOSELAND	GBR	HM Plant Ducati	Ducati 998 F 01	21	38'54.814	37.490		15 1'50.319
7	7	P. CHILI	ITA	Ducati NCR Axo	Ducati 998 RS	21	38'58.724	41.400		15 1'50.403
8	10	G. LAVILLA	ESP	Alstare Suzuki Corona	Suzuki GSX-R750 Y	21	39'00.125	42.801		15 1'50.303
9	12	B. PARKES	AUS	Ducati NCR Parmalat	Ducati 998 RS	21	39'00.320	42.996		15 1'50.437
10	155	B. BOSTROM	USA	Ducati L & M	Ducati 998 F 02	21	39'06.705	49.381		9 1'50.931
11	9	C. WALKER	GBR	Kawasaki Racing	Kawasaki ZX-7RR	21	39'10.780	53.456		15 1'50.836
12	30	A. ANTONELLO	ITA	DFX Racing Ducati Pirelli	Ducati 998 RS	21	39'19.875	1'02.551		17 1'50.973
13	99	S. MARTIN	AUS	DFX Racing Ducati Pirelli	Ducati 998 RS	21	39'22.286	1'04.962		17 1'50.988
14	19	L. PEDERCINI	ITA	Pedercini	Ducati 998 RS	21	39'22.797	1'05.473		15 1'50.790
15	14	H. IZUTSU	JPN	Kawasaki Racing	Kawasaki ZX-7RR	21	39'26.191	1'08.867		16 1'51.089
16	20	M. BORCIANI	ITA	Pedercini	Ducati 998 RS	21	39'40.207	1'22.883		16 1'51.737
17	46	M. SANCHINI	ITA	Kawasaki Bertocchi	Kawasaki ZX-7RR	21	40'02.721	1'45.397		16 1'52.748
18	36	I. CLEMENTI	ITA	Kawasaki Bertocchi	Kawasaki ZX-7RR	21	40'11.727	1'54.403		15 1'53.681
19	50	A. VALIA	ITA	Ass. Sportiva Bassani	Ducati 996 RS	21	40'24.870	2'07.546		13 1'54.086
20	5	M. HECKLES	GBR	Castrol Honda Rumi	Honda VTR 1000 SP2	21	40'31.371	2'14.047		16 1'54.080
21	113	P. BLORA	ITA	Pacific	Ducati 996 RS	21	40'32.629	2'15.305		18 1'54.456
22	77	R. ASSIRELLI	ITA	Pirelli	Yamaha R7	20	40'44.346	1 Lap		15 1'59.374

---Not Classified:---

	No.	Rider	Nat	Team	Bike	Laps	Time	Gap	Speed	Fastest Lap
RET	60	J. VIDAL	ESP	White Endurance	Honda VTR 1000 SP1	13	27'27.818	8 Laps		6 1'54.863
RET	75	L. PINI	ITA	Pedercini	Ducati 996 RS	11	21'19.850	10 Laps		3 1'54.041
RET	6	P. GODDARD	AUS	Benelli Sport	Benelli Tornado 900	9	17'06.622	12 Laps		5 1'52.950
RET	151	M. MALATESTA	ITA	Pro.Con.	Ducati 996 RS	9	17'14.371	12 Laps		8 1'53.921
RET	28	S. FOTI	ITA	Pedercini	Ducati 996 RS	8	16'09.599	13 Laps		4 1'54.051
RET	33	J. BORJA	ESP	Spaziotel Racing	Ducati 998 RS	6	11'48.719	15 Laps		5 1'51.795

RACE 2

Laps 21 = 103,593 km - Avg. 162,631 km/h

	No.	Rider	Nat	Team	Bike	Laps	Time	Gap	Speed	Fastest Lap
1	2	C. EDWARDS	USA	Castrol Honda	Honda VTR 1000 SP2	21	38'13.128		263,7	20 1'48.457
2	1	T. BAYLISS	AUS	Ducati Infostrada	Ducati 998 F 02	21	38'14.108	0.980	266,9	13 1'48.389
3	11	R. XAUS	ESP	Ducati Infostrada	Ducati 998 F 02	21	38'19.311	6.183	266,3	11 1'48.741
4	41	N. HAGA	JPN	Playstation2-FGF Aprilia	Aprilia RSV 1000	21	38'34.775	21.647	264,3	2 1'49.292
5	100	N. HODGSON	GBR	HM Plant Ducati	Ducati 998 F 01	21	38'40.531	27.403	264,3	5 1'49.382
6	52	J. TOSELAND	GBR	HM Plant Ducati	Ducati 998 F 01	21	38'47.315	34.187	249,7	3 1'50.375
7	10	G. LAVILLA	ESP	Alstare Suzuki Corona	Suzuki GSX-R750 Y	21	38'54.737	41.609	253,2	3 1'50.178
8	12	B. PARKES	AUS	Ducati NCR Parmalat	Ducati 998 RS	21	38'54.947	41.819	241,3	14 1'50.459
9	155	B. BOSTROM	USA	Ducati L & M	Ducati 998 F 02	21	39'02.514	49.386	253,2	4 1'50.674
10	14	H. IZUTSU	JPN	Kawasaki Racing	Kawasaki ZX-7RR	21	39'04.351	51.223	255,0	6 1'50.540
11	33	J. BORJA	ESP	Spaziotel Racing	Ducati 998 RS	21	39'04.546	51.418	253,8	20 1'50.848
12	9	C. WALKER	GBR	Kawasaki Racing	Kawasaki ZX-7RR	21	39'36.342	1'23.214	248,5	19 1'51.540
13	19	L. PEDERCINI	ITA	Pedercini	Ducati 998 RS	21	39'39.908	1'26.780	252,0	8 1'51.002
14	99	S. MARTIN	AUS	DFX Racing Ducati Pirelli	Ducati 998 RS	21	39'52.377	1'39.249	260,5	9 1'52.010
15	46	M. SANCHINI	ITA	Kawasaki Bertocchi	Kawasaki ZX-7RR	21	39'59.777	1'46.649	250,3	2 1'53.383
16	36	I. CLEMENTI	ITA	Kawasaki Bertocchi	Kawasaki ZX-7RR	21	40'01.968	1'48.840	241,3	3 1'53.563
17	50	A. VALIA	ITA	Ass. Sportiva Bassani	Ducati 996 RS	20	38'21.478	1 Lap	242,9	2 1'53.869
18	60	J. VIDAL	ESP	White Endurance	Honda VTR 1000 SP1	20	38'43.693	1 Lap	246,8	8 1'54.637
19	77	R. ASSIRELLI	ITA	Pirelli	Yamaha R7	18	38'26.225	3 Laps	230,5	4 1'57.933

---Not Classified:---

	No.	Rider	Nat	Team	Bike	Laps	Time	Gap	Speed	Fastest Lap
RET	28	S. FOTI	ITA	Pedercini	Ducati 996 RS	19	36'15.082	2 Laps	255,6	3 1'53.499
RET	75	L. PINI	ITA	Pedercini	Ducati 996 RS	18	34'58.382	3 Laps	250,8	5 1'54.022
RET	7	P. CHILI	ITA	Ducati NCR Axo	Ducati 998 RS	17	31'27.663	4 Laps	257,4	15 1'50.448
RET	20	M. BORCIANI	ITA	Pedercini	Ducati 998 RS	16	30'18.766	5 Laps	257,4	6 1'51.670
RET	5	M. HECKLES	GBR	Castrol Honda Rumi	Honda VTR 1000 SP2	12	24'03.061	9 Laps	241,9	8 1'54.224
RET	151	M. MALATESTA	ITA	Pro.Con.	Ducati 996 RS	8	16'03.060	13 Laps	256,8	4 1'54.112
RET	113	P. BLORA	ITA	Pacific	Ducati 996 RS	2	4'04.227	19 Laps	222,4	2 2'04.111
RET	30	A. ANTONELLO	ITA	DFX Racing Ducati Pirelli	Ducati 998 RS	1	2'20.743	20 Laps	208,3	

SUPERSPORT
WORLD CHAMPIONSHIP

SUPERSPORT

FABIEN, THE CHAMPION (99)

The nickname 'FGV'(Foret Grande Vitesse, coined after the French Railways TGV high-speed train) is just right for a rider who has earned considerable praise from his engineers and his rivals out on the track. Fabien achieved the biggest win of his career, the World Supersport crown, at the age of 29, ten years after his first race. Born on January 29th 1973 at Angouleme (but he lives with Florence in Aix-en-Provence), Fabien made his debut in 1992 at Le Mans in the Yamaha TZR Cup 125 and immediately won his first race! Three years later he moved up into 600 on a Ducati 748 and in 1997 took part with scarce results in the Promosport 1000 championship.

However Foret found support to race in the national Superbike championship with a Yamaha R1 'Stocksport', with which he was able to win the final round of 1998. At this point Yamaha Motor France gave him a factory team bike for the same category, in which he finished runner-up. In 2000 Yamaha again called him up to race in Endurance, and Foret won at Spa and at the Bol d'Or together with Willis and Deletang. That season he had his first contact with the world of Supersport, making his debut with a Team De Cecco Ducati 748 at

Oschersleben, but the limited budget of the Italian team was a halt to his performances. In 2001 he joined the Dutch team, Ten Kate, alongside Pere Riba and the results were immediately promising, Foret winning two of the last three rounds of the season. The rest is history: the Frenchman was promoted to leading rider when his Spanish team-mate moved (with disappointing results) to MotoGP, but already in the first round at Valencia, 'FGV' had made clear his intentions by winning from Chambon. He controlled the situation well in the following rounds with a series of good results and then took a well-deserved win

at the high-speed Monza track. His season took an unexpected twist at the Lausitzring round, when his Honda was disqualified after the rear wheel hub was found to be lighter than what had been declared on the bike's homologation papers. Foret however remained focussed and picked up a clear win at the following round, Misano Adriatico. He scored points in every round of the championship and clinched the title by winning at Assen and controlling his rivals at Imola. Crazy about cycling, climbing, golf

SUPERSPORT

and motocross, Fabien considers the Supersport title he has just won as merely the next stage in a career inspired by his idol Kevin Schwantz. Some of the credit for Foret's title however must also go to the bike the newly-crowned world champion sat on throughout the season - the Honda CBR 600 FS, an extremely quick four-cylinder machine prepared by Dutch expert Gerrit ten Kate and his son Ronald. Just under twenty people make up the team, which as well as Foret also

WORLD CHAMPIONSHIP

entered the experienced Scot Ian McPherson (ninth overall). Support from Pirelli tyres was also important, with the Italian manufacturer providing some excellent Supercorsa radials for the French champion.

SUPERSPORT

KATSUAKI FUJIWARA (37)
STEPHANE CHAMBON (12)

The 'twins' of the Alstare-Suzuki Corona Extra team were two of the stars of the 2002 World Supersport Championship, winning four races between them. Three went to 27 year-old Fujiwara, who tried to keep the title from going into French hands right down to the wire. Maybe without his DNFs at Valencia and Kyalami, he might have succeeded. For his part, veteran Frenchman Stephane Chambon was still competitive at 37 years of age, and almost always finished in the points, even leading the championship on one occasion. His Brands Hatch crash however meant that he lost ground on the leaders. The Suzuki GSX-R of the two riders, who finished second and third in the table, was once again extremely competitive in the hands of the Belgian-Japanese team headed by Francesco Batta.

PAOLO CASOLI (2)

Another 'veteran' who continues to race with great determination and courage, 'Gasolio' only won once, at Oschersleben, but was always up amongst the front-runners. After twenty years in racing, Casoli, on a team Belgarda Yamaha R6, was one of the contenders for the title, but again just missed the target.

JAMIE WHITHAM (69)

One year younger than his team-mate and, like Casoli, he also won one round of the championship. Not very competitive in qualifying, Jamie always gave 110% in the races, as demonstrated by his high crash rate. This year he was also sidelined by numerous technical problems.

WORLD CHAMPIONSHIP

CHRISTIAN KELLNER (91)

In his third year of World Supersport, the 21 year-old German from the Yamaha Motor Germany team finished sixth overall in the championship. One podium finish was somewhat of a disappointment for Kellner after his excellent season in 2000, and in particular 2001.

JORG TEUCHERT (3)

The other Yamaha Germany rider, 2000 Supersport champion, had again been expected to challenge for the title, but the 22 year-old from Lasf a.d. Pegnitz had to settle for eighth overall in the standings. Teuchert had quite a good season, but he was not as competitive as in the previous years, when he won (2000) and finished third (2001).

ANDREW PITT (1)

After a superb start to the season, the reigning world champion had a few disappointing races which excluded him from the final title run-in. His bike, the Kawasaki ZX-6R, was not one of the candidates for victory, but the Australian demonstrated that it is still very competitive in the right hands.

CHRIS VERMEULEN (17)

20 year-old Vermeulen is one of the best young talents in Supersport. After making his debut in 2000, the Australian immediately sprung to the attention of the Supersport teams for his ability. He twice finished on the podium with a Van Zon Honda (a satellite team of Ten Kate).

WORLD CHAMPIONSHIP

ALESSIO CORRADI (15)

The surprise of the season after showing what he could do as a 'wild-card' rider in 2001. In his first full year on the world stage, the 26 year-old from Parma showed great ability, and can only improve with more experience.

KEVIN CURTAIN (5)

A late addition to World Supersport (he was called in to replace McPherson a few days before the first round at Valencia), the 36 year-old Australian did the best he could with a Yamaha R6 of the Austrian OPCM team).

PIERGIORGIO BONTEMPI (11)

After a podium at Phillip Island, the 34 year-old from Ancona was looking forward to a positive season, but the NCR-prepared Ducati 748 failed to live up to expectations.

SUPERSPORT

VALENCIA

Winter testing confirmed that Supersport is an extremely competitive and hard-fought category. In the first race of the season, Frenchman Fabien Foret (Honda) immediately proved to be the man to beat after a terrific battle with Stephane Chambon (Suzuki), the only rider capable of keeping the pace of the leader, helped by superb Pirelli tyres. The other riders who had a good race included the young Australian Chris Vermeulen (Honda) and Italy's Alessio Corradi (Yamaha).

WORLD CHAMPIONSHIP

PHILLIP ISLAND

Paolo Casoli ruined a superb race with a crash on the last lap, leaving the win to the reigning world champion, Australian Andrew Pitt, who knows the circuit like the back of his hand. Behind the Kawasaki rider finished a rejuvenated Piergiorgio Bontempi (Ducati) and the Alstare-Suzuki pairing of Chambon and Fujiwara. Foret failed to finish higher than ninth place after a contact with another rider but did not lose too many points to the new leader.

KYALAMI

Kawasaki might have the oldest bike in the field (the 636 is not eligible for Supersport races), but Pitt didn't seem to notice as he powered to his second successive win in the world championship. His rivals James Whitham (lap record) and Stephane Chambon finished with him on the podium. Foret scored another finish, but the points gap to Pitt was now increasing. Teuchert and Kellner, Yamaha's two German riders, continued to notch up the points and were now second and fourth in the championship.

SUGO

The Suzuki-Alstare team was the one to beat at the Japanese circuit and the result was a foregone conclusion: Chambon and Fujiwara scored a 1-2 and the Frenchman moved into the lead of the championship. Pitt, who had dominated the early races, could only manage a seventh place after a weekend full of problems. The podium in Japan was completed by Foret, who with his Honda-Pirelli, settled for third after vainly chasing after the leading duo, while Paolo Casoli finished fourth.

SUPERSPORT

MONZA

All eyes were on Foret at Monza after a crash in Friday qualifying. On Sunday however the Frenchman was fully-focussed and went on to win the race, taking over second place in the championship just a few points behind leader Chambon. The star at Monza however was the young Australian Chris Vermeulen, who set pole position and kept Foret busy right to the chequered flag. Another superb battle was between Fujiwara and Pitt, while Chambon finished fifth. Eight riders were involved in a fantastic slipstreaming battle in the early laps, confirming Monza to be the fastest track on the WSBK calendar.

WORLD CHAMPIONSHIP

SILVERSTONE

The rain gave the first win of the season to Yamaha-Belgarda, but it was a lucky win because both Whitham and Casoli crashed while they were leading on the very lap the red flags were brought out to mark the end of the rain-affected race. The results were declared valid at the end of the previous lap, so the win went to the British rider followed by his team-mate. Karl Muggeridge had a more prudent ride to finish third. Three points now separated Chambon and Foret at the top of the standings.

LAUSITZ

Foret saw his Lausitz win taken away from him for a technical irregularity, so the maximum points went to Fujiwara, who finished ahead of reigning world champion Andrew Pitt and Stephane Chambon. Failing to get their bikes to restart in parc fermé also meant the exclusion of both Whitham and Casoli, who were respectively seventh and tenth. Chambon increased his championship lead over his chief rival, who was now Pitt after Foret's problems; the other Alstare-Suzuki rider, Fujiwara, was also catching up with the leaders in the points table.

MISANO

The Misano round brought things back to normal with a superb win for Foret, who moved back into the lead of the points table. A photo-finish separated the winner from second-placed Fujiwara, who was rapidly gaining on the leaders. The podium was completed by Jamie Whitham, with a result that gave some satisfaction to team Yamaha-Belgarda. Disappointment however for Chambon, who crashed while in the lead in an attempt to force the pace. Paolo Casoli could only finish fifth in his home race after a wrong tyre choice.

SUPERSPORT

BRANDS HATCH

A series of crashes forced the Supersport race to be interrupted several times. One rider who finished on the tarmac was Stephane Chambon, who now looked as if he had to say goodbye to the championship. Fujiwara, Foret and Casoli had to keep one eye on the aggregate times in the four parts of the race and in the end it was the Japanese rider who took the win. The 25 points moved him into second place in the standings, behind Foret, while third place was a boost in confidence for Paolo Casoli.

OSCHERSLEBEN

Foret was also making news off the track with the announcement of his move to Kawasaki, but in the race he crashed while in the lead, only to remount again and finish fifth. The win finally went to Paolo Casoli, who beat off the attacks of Chambon and Fujiwara in a superb finish. These three were the only survivors in a ten-strong group of riders who provided all the excitement in the early laps. With fourth place, Pitt kept in touch with the championship leaders.

ASSEN

Assen produced another exciting race, but it was interrupted five laps from the end when Kellner's Yamaha engine blew in a big way and dumped oil all over the track. The results on the previous lap stood, meaning that Foret took the win to move closer to the title, while MacPherson and Casoli were second and third. The spectacular crash on the oil saw six riders involved but luckily no one was hurt. Fujiwara, one of the candidates for the title, was fifth, while Chambon was ninth. Pitt crashed after making contact with Corradi.

WORLD CHAMPIONSHIP

IMOLA

Foret (Honda) and Fujiwara (Suzuki) were the two favourites for the title and the Frenchman started the race from pole position. The Japanese rider was up for the battle and took the lead at the start, followed by Corradi, who was then forced to retire. Victory in the final race of the season for Fujiwara wasn't enough however because Foret played it safe in fifth place, which was enough to give him the world title. The podium was completed by Chambon (Suzuki) and Vermeulen (Honda), while another of the season's protagonists, Andrew Pitt, retired almost immediately.

SUPERSPORT

RIDERS

	Points	Points From First	Points From Previous	March 10 SPAIN	March 24 AUSTRALIA	April 7 SOUTH AFRICA	April 21 JAPAN	May 12 ITALY 1	May 26 GREAT BRITAIN	June 9 GERMANY 1	June 23 SAN MARINO	July 28 EUROPE	September 1 GERMANY 2	September 8 NETHERLANDS	September 29 ITALY 2
1 FORET	186			25	7	11	16	25	9		25	20	10	25	13
				1	3	3	3	2	2	3	1	1	1	1	1
2 FUJIWARA	181	5			13		20	16	10	25	20	25	16	11	25
					8	12	5	4	5	4	4	2	2	2	2
3 CHAMBON	162	24	19	20	16	16	25	11	8	16	3		20	7	20
				2	1	2	1	1	1	1	2	3	3	3	3
4 CASOLI	128	58	34	8		9	13	10	20		11	16	25	16	
				8	12	10	6	7	4	6	6	6	5	4	4
5 PITT	126	60	2	11	25	25	9	13		20	10		13		
				5	1	1	2	3	3	2	3	4	4	5	5
6 KELLNER	94	92	32	16	10	10	11		5	13	13	10		6	
				3	4	4	4	5	7	5	5	5	6	6	6
7 VERMEULEN	90	96	4	13	5	7		20	2	11	8	8			16
				4	6	7	11	6	9	8	8	7	7	9	7
8 TEUCHERT	90	96	0		11	13	6	7	13	10		11		8	11
					9	8	9	9	8	6	9	8	8	8	7
9 MACPHERSON	83	103	7		8	8		8	11	6		13		20	9
					12	11	13	12	11	11	11	10	10	9	9
10 WHITHAM	80	106	3	10		20			25		16			9	
				6	10	5	6	10	6	9	6	8	8	7	10
11 CURTAIN	56	130	24		4		7			9	5	7	11	13	
					17	18	16	16	16	15	14	14	13	11	11
12 CORRADI	56	130	0	9	6	6	5			5	6	9	8	2	
				7	7	9	10	11	13	13	12	12	10	11	11
13 BONTEMPI	51	135	5	5	20	5		9		7	2			3	
				11	5	5	6	8	10	10	10	11	12	13	13
14 MUGGERIDGE	43	143	8	2		3	10		16	2				10	
				14	19	17	14	14	12	12	13	13	14	14	14
15 COGAN	34	152	9		9	4					9			5	7
					11	12	15	15	15	17	16	17	17	16	15
16 CRUCIANI	31	155	3				2		4	8	4	5			8
							22	24	21	16	17	16	16	17	16
17 DAEMEN	29	157	2	6	2	2	8	6				4		1	
				10	12	14	12	12	14	14	15	15	15	15	17
18 ULM	25	161	4	3	3					4	7			4	4
				13	16	16	18	19	21	20	18	18	18	18	18
19 CARLACCI	20	166	5	7			1	2							10
				9	15	15	17	17	19	20	21	21	22	22	19
20 ELLISON	20	166	0	1	1		3				3		7		5
				15	19	20	19	20	23	23	23	23	19	19	19
21 LAGRIVE	18	168	2					5	6				4		3
								20	16	18	19	19	19	19	21
22 NANNELLI	12	174	6	4				4	3				1		
				12	17	18	20	18	16	18	19	19	21	21	22
23 GIUGOVAZ	10	176	2					3	7						
								23	19	20	21	21	22	22	23
24 HANSON	9	177	1										9		
													24	24	24

First Line: Championship Standings - Second Line: Ranking Progression

144

R I D E R S

	Points	Points From First	Points From Previous	March 10 SPAIN	March 24 AUSTRALIA	April 7 SOUTH AFRICA	April 21 JAPAN	May 12 ITALY 1	May 26 GREAT BRITAIN	June 9 GERMANY 1	June 23 SAN MARINO	July 28 EUROPE	September 1 GERMANY 2	September 8 NETHERLANDS	September 29 ITALY 2
25 FROST	6	180	3												6 / 25
26 OELSCHLAGER	6	180	0										6 / 25	25	25
27 EASTON	6	180	0									6 / 24	25	25	25
28 CHARPENTIER	6	180	0					1 / 25	25	26	26	2 / 26	3 / 25	25	25
29 BRIAN	5	181	1									5 / 28		28	29
30 DE GEA	5	181	0				4 / 20	22	24	1 / 23	23	25	28	28	29
31 MCGUINNESS	4	182	1						1 / 25	26	26	1 / 28	2 / 30	30	31
32 ZAISER	3	183	1							3 / 25	25	26	31	31	32
33 YOUNG	2	184	1												2 / 33
34 LAVERTY	1	185	1												1 / 34
35 MARIOTTINI	1	185	0								1 / 26	29	32	32	34
36 MOODLEY	1	185	0			1 / 21	23	25	25	26	26	29	32	32	34

First Line: Championship Standings   -   Second Line: Ranking Progression

M A N U F A C T U R E S

	Points	Points From First	Points From Previous	March 10 SPAIN	March 24 AUSTRALIA	April 7 SOUTH AFRICA	April 21 JAPAN	May 12 ITALY 1	May 26 GREAT BRITAIN	June 9 GERMANY 1	June 23 SAN MARINO	July 28 EUROPE	September 1 GERMANY 2	September 8 NETHERLANDS	September 29 ITALY 2
1 SUZUKI	229			20 / 2	16 / 1	16 / 2	25 / 1	16 / 1	10 / 1	25 / 1	20 / 1	25 / 1	20 / 1	11 / 1	25 / 1
2 HONDA	209	20		25 / 1	9 / 3	11 / 4	16 / 3	25 / 2	16 / 2	11 / 2	25 / 2	20 / 2	10 / 2	25 / 2	16 / 2
3 YAMAHA	192	37	17	16 / 3	11 / 4	20 / 3	13 / 4	10 / 4	25 / 3	13 / 3	16 / 3	16 / 3	25 / 3	16 / 3	11 / 3
4 KAWASAKI	134	95	58	11 / 4	25 / 1	25 / 1	9 / 2	13 / 3		20 / 4	10 / 4	3 / 4	13 / 4	/ 4	5 / 4
5 DUCATI	61	168	73	5 / 5	20 / 5	5 / 5	/ 5	9 / 5	3 / 5	7 / 5	2 / 5	6 / 5	1 / 5	3 / 5	5 / 5

First Line: Championship Standings   -   Second Line: Ranking Progression

EUROPEAN CHAMPIONSHIP

Despite his youthful appearance, European Superstock champion, 20 year-old Vittorio Iannuzzo from Avellino made his motorcycle racing debut at the age of 14 in 1996. The Italian immediately proved his potential, stepping up to World Supersport in 1999 with a Yamaha, but there he accumulated experience and little else.

A desire to show his true potential saw him moving this year to Sueprstock, after accepting an offer from Suzuki who put him into the Alstare-Suzuki Italia team led by ex-rider Fabrizio Pirovano. After the support from Vittorio's father Armando, it was 'Piro' who proved to be the catalyst in Iannuzzo's career: he persuaded him to move up north and followed his young protégé in both his physical and race training. The results came immediately: a win at Valencia, another at Monza, a careful race in difficult conditions at Silverstone, then another win at Lausitz. At the mid-point in the championship, Iannuzzo had almost twice the number of points as his closest rival, but his desire to win remained the same, as he proved at Misano. Despite being beaten by fellow-Italian Vizziello, he put up a good fight right to the very end. His season took an incredible twist at Brands Hatch, where he was unable to avoid a rider who fell in front of him, breaking his left femur and right collarbone in the crash. With a prognosis

of two months, everyone thought Iannuzzo's season was over, except for Vittorio who courageously underwent intensive therapy and despite incredible pain got back on the bike again at Oschersleben thirty days later! In that race he set fourth quickest time in qualifying and at the chequered flag was fifth, a position that enabled him to hold on to his championship lead. He had another superb race at Assen one week later and then stepped onto the top of the podium once again in the season's Imola finale.

Iannuzzo, a rider from the south of Italy (an area that produces few motorbike champions), scored four wins in 2002 but above all demonstrated real character in his European title-winning season.

The battle for the runner-up position was between two more Italians, 24 year-old Walter Tortoroglio from Piedmont and 22 year-old Gianluca Vizziello from

Matera. The former, European Superstock runner-up in 2001, ran out of steam in the final two rounds of the season. His Rumi Honda CBR 1000 RR might not have been as quick as Iannuzzo's GSX-R 1000, but "Tortorix" never once gave up and even managed to win at Oschersleben. Vizziello, in his second year in Superstock, with a GIMotorsport Yamaha R1, was third overall but could have been higher in the standings had he not been disqualified for technical reasons after the German round in September. Gianluca's win at Misano was the highlight of his year.
Two more young Italians were also well-placed in the final championship

standings: 19 year-old Giacomo Romanelli, who was fifth on the second Alstare-Suzuki and 22 year-old Lorenzo Alfonsi, who was sixth on a DFX Ducati.

Moving away from Italy, two more riders to watch were the 24 year-old British rider Charlie Burns, who won his two home rounds, and Belgium's Koen Vleugels, also 24 years of age. Both riders were on the almost unbeatable Suzuki GSX-R 1000 (seven wins in nine races). Another British rider, Michael Laverty, on a team EMS Suzuki, won at Assen, while the best non-Italian rider was another Brit, Alan Notman, who finished fourth overall with a LiveOnScreen Suzuki.

151

FINAL CHAMPIONSHIP STANDINGS

1°	V.	Iannuzzo (ITA)	Suzuki	p. 152
2°	W.	Tortoroglio (ITA)	Honda	p. 103
3°	G.L.	Vizziello (ITA)	Yamaha	p. 100
4°	A.	Notman (GBR)	Suzuki	p. 83
5°	G.	Romanelli (ITA)	Suzuki	p. 71
6°	L.	Alfonsi (ITA)	Ducati	p. 71
7°	K.	Vleugels (BEL)	Suzuki	p. 54
8°	C.	Burns (GBR)	Suzuki	p. 50
9°	D.	Vankeymeul (BEL)	Suzuki	p. 49
10°	R.	Chiarello (ITA)	Ducati	p. 42
11°	S.	Brogan (GBR)	Suzuki	p. 36
12°	K.	Murphy (GBR)	Suzuki	p. 36
13°	L.	Mauri (ITA)	Yamaha	p. 32
14°	L.	Forreau (FRA)	Suzuki	p. 29
15°	A.	Martinez (ESP)	Suzuki	p. 28
16°	I.	Dionisi (ITA)	Yamaha	p. 26
17°	B.	Nabert (GER)	Suzuki	p. 26
18°	A.	Brannetti (ITA)	Honda	p. 26
19°	M.	Laverty (GBR)	Suzuki	p. 25
20°	O.	Four (FRA)	Suzuki	p. 23

followed by other teams.

SUPERSIDE
WORLD CHAMPIONSHIP

ORLD CHAMPIONSHIP

Five riders had a chance of winning the 2002 title at the start of the final Imola round of the season: all of them were important names in the history of the three-wheeled category.

The season had got underway with four different winners in the first five races: Abbott-Biggs at Valencia and Silverstone, Webster-Woodhead at Kyalami, world champions Klaffenbock-Parzer, who won the Monza round, and Steinhausen-Hopkins, who triumphed at Lausitz. Thanks to a series of good results, Hanks-P.Biggs also managed to get into the leading battle.

At that point the title battle appeared to be between Steinhausen, Abbott and Hanks, but Webster-Woodhead's win at Brands (followed by wins at Oschersleben and Assen), together with Klaffenbock's consistent finishing, threw the title race wide open.

So at the start of the Imola race, it was now a five-way battle: between leader Abbott and fifth-placed Klaffenbock there were only 19 points.

SUPERSIDE

W

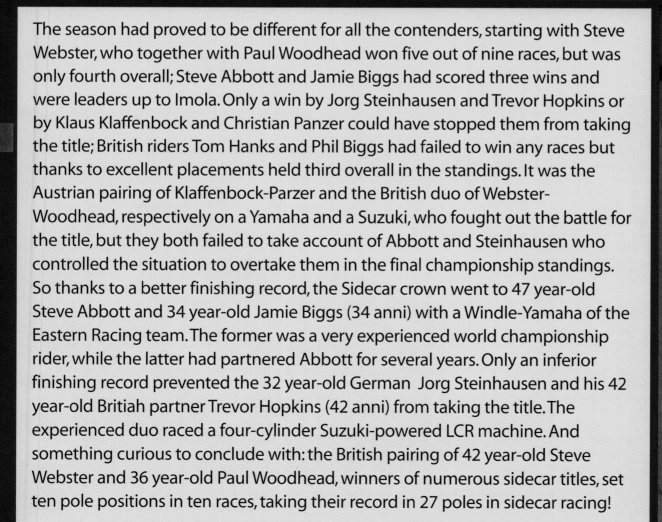

The season had proved to be different for all the contenders, starting with Steve Webster, who together with Paul Woodhead won five out of nine races, but was only fourth overall; Steve Abbott and Jamie Biggs had scored three wins and were leaders up to Imola. Only a win by Jorg Steinhausen and Trevor Hopkins or by Klaus Klaffenbock and Christian Panzer could have stopped them from taking the title; British riders Tom Hanks and Phil Biggs had failed to win any races but thanks to excellent placements held third overall in the standings. It was the Austrian pairing of Klaffenbock-Parzer and the British duo of Webster-Woodhead, respectively on a Yamaha and a Suzuki, who fought out the battle for the title, but they both failed to take account of Abbott and Steinhausen who controlled the situation to overtake them in the final championship standings. So thanks to a better finishing record, the Sidecar crown went to 47 year-old Steve Abbott and 34 year-old Jamie Biggs (34 anni) with a Windle-Yamaha of the Eastern Racing team. The former was a very experienced world championship rider, while the latter had partnered Abbott for several years. Only an inferior finishing record prevented the 32 year-old German Jorg Steinhausen and his 42 year-old Britiah partner Trevor Hopkins (42 anni) from taking the title. The experienced duo raced a four-cylinder Suzuki-powered LCR machine. And something curious to conclude with: the British pairing of 42 year-old Steve Webster and 36 year-old Paul Woodhead, winners of numerous sidecar titles, set ten pole positions in ten races, taking their record in 27 poles in sidecar racing!

SIDECAR

FINAL CHAMPIONSHIP STANDINGS

1°	S. Abbott - J. Biggs (GBR/GBR)	Yamaha	p. 151
2°	J. Steinhausen - T. Hopkins (GER/GBR)	Suzuki	p. 151
3°	K. Klaffenbock – C. Parzer (GER/GBR)	Yamaha	p. 146
4°	S. Webster – P. Woodhead (GBR/GBR)	Suzuki	p. 145
5°	T. Hanks – P. Biggs (GBR/GBR)	Yamaha	p. 145
6°	M. Schlosser – A. Hanni (SUI/SUI)	Suzuki	p. 98
7°	M. Van Gils – C. Buyserd (NED/NED)	Suzuki	p. 69
8°	G. Hauzenberger – T. Crone (AUT/GBR)	Suzuki	p. 61
9°	P. Schroeder – U. Wafker (SUI/SUI)	Suzuki	p. 60
10°	R. Lovelock – G. Yendell (GBR/GBR)	Suzuki	p. 48
11°	U. Gottlich – J. Koloska (GER/GER)	Suzuki	p. 47
12°	S. Muldoon – A. Peach (GBR/GBR)	Suzuki	p. 39
13°	C. Founds – P. Founds (GBR/GBR)	Yamaha	p. 29
14°	R. Cameron – I. Simons (GBR/GBR)	Suzuki	p. 25
15°	S. Delannoy – J. Vannier (FRA/FRA)	Suzuki	p. 25

followed by 13 other teams.